WHY THE VILLAGE MOVEMENT?

FOREWORD

To the Third Edition

It is a good sign that **"Why The Village Movement ?"** is required to go through the third edition. It supplies a felt want. Prof. J. C. Kumarappa answers almost all the doubts that have been expressed about the necessity and feasibility of the movement. No lover of villages can afford to be without the booklet. No doubter can fail to have his doubts dispelled. It is of no use to those who have made up their minds that the only movement worth the name is to destroy the villages and dot India with a number of big cities where highly centralized industries will be carried out and every one will have plenty and to spare. Fortunately as yet there are not many who belong to that school of destruction. I wonder if the Village Movement has come just in time to prevent the spread of the movement of despair. This booklet is an attempt to answer the question.

Segaon-Wardha
2-2-39

M. K. Gandhi

PREFACE

Preface to the First Edition :

Amongst thinking people the world over there is a growing dissatisfaction as to the efficacy of capitalism as a cure for the poverty that faces us. Industrialization depends on the guarantee of a steady flow of raw materials and a ready market for manufactured goods. The system, therefore, requires as a pre-requisite a control of raw materials and markets which can only be obtained by violence. Soviet Communism, while seeking to remove the profit motive, has retained centralized production which entails concentration of power and, hence, calls for a greater sense of trusteeship to administer it for the benefit of the masses than is required under concentration of wealth. Ultimately, the difficulties of collection of raw materials and distribution of finished goods will have to be faced. Both capitalism and communism are based on a consideration of material values forgetting that such a myth as the "Economic Man" does not exist. The human factor and the effects of culture are ignored.

In this booklet it is sought to examine the chances of basing an economic order on cultural values and human needs which formed the foundation of the old Oriental Civilization, Man is a complex being. We cannot nurture him to his full stature under a system which carries division of labour to the extreme. His religion, philosophy, politics, social and economic activities, and his family relations have all to be rolled into one before a cultural person can evolve. We cannot segregate various aspects of his life in different compartments and attempt to develop them in distinct stages.

The practical side of the theme of this booklet can be seen in the programme of work of the All India Spinners' Association and the All India Village Industries Association. If this booklet clarifies to some extent the ideals of these Associations it will justify its existence.

Maganwadi,
Wardha, C. P.
21-12-36

J. C. Kumarappa

WHY THE VILLAGE MOVEMENT?

[A Plea for a Village Centred Economic Order in India]

BY

J. C. KUMARAPPA

GYAN

Published by

Gyan Publishing House
5, Ansari Road
Daryaganj, New Delhi-110002
Phone: 011-47034999, 9811692060
E-mail: books@gyanbooks.com

Distribution Network
gyanbooks.com
India, USA, Canada, UK, Australia

ISBN: 978-93-6208-004-2 (PB)
First Published, 1936

2nd Impression 2024

Printed at: Gyan Press, Delhi.

WHY THE VILLAGE MOVEMENT?
Author: J. C. KUMARAPPA

WHY THE VILLAGE MOVEMENT?

WHY THE VILLAGE MOVEMENT ?

[A Plea for a Village Centred Economic Order in India]

BY

J. C. KUMARAPPA

With a foreword

BY

MAHATMA GANDHI

Preface to the Fourth Edition :

The manuscript of this edition was ready for the press in 1942, nearly three years ago; but its publication had been delayed by the detention and subsequent incarceration of the author under the Defence of India Rules. During this interval great events have taken place on the stage of world history, supporting and demonstrating in a practical manner much of the arguments adduced in this book in favour of decentralization. The alignment of Russia with the Imperialistic forces of Great Britain and the United States of America incontrovertibly proves that centralization of industries is inimical to the development of democracy in politics. Indeed dictatorships are but the counterparts of cartels and monopolies in economics, being merely a variant of the same psychological approach manifested in different spheres. Opinion is also fast veering round that being armed to the teeth is no guarantee of Peace or Freedom. Under such circumstances there is a temptation at every stage to repeat "I told you so." Though the thesis of this book is abundantly proved by such external evidence, we venture to place this edition once again before the public as the theme is of perennial interest.

The text of this edition has been amplified by the addition of chapters on "Schools of Economies", "Peoples' Income" "Moral Issues of Riches", "Non-violent Standard of Life" and "Planned Economy."

We are grateful to the Hindustan Publishing Co., Ltd, Rajahmundry, the publishers of the first three editions, for granting us permission to bring out this edition. We are also under obligation to Syt. Madhav Satavalekar for the interesting design of the dust cover.

Maganwadi,
Wardha, C. P.
22-2-45 — **J. C. Kumarappa**

Preface to the Fifth Edition :

Barring the addition of a few explanatory paragraphs in a few chapters not much has been altered in this edition.

Maganwadi,
Wardha, C. P.
24-6-48 — **J. C. Kumarappa**

CONTENTS

PART I

Historical Background

PART II

The Modern Situation

CHAPTER V

CHAPTER VI

CHAPTER VII

PAGES

PART I

HISTORICAL BACKGROUND

CHAPTER I STAGES OF EVOLUTION

The Animal Kingdom :

In the most primitive stages of both men and animals economic activity is the result of an urge to satisfy primary needs, such as :

1. Hunger.
2. Protection against natural elements like wind and weather.
3. Protection against outside attack.

The most elementary form of economic activity is that of gathering supplies which exist in nature. A monkey feels hungry, it stretches out its hand and plucks the leaf or fruit. This is purely predatory. The monkey has done nothing to produce the leaf or fruit. If any factor intervenes which is likely to prevent or retard the supply satisfying the demand, friction is at once generated and causes heat or violence. Thus, if a hungry dog is prevented from consuming the bone he is eating, at once there is violence.

In this activity the animal is highly self-centred and individualistic. If a species is gregarious at all, they get together for hunting down their prey like wolves in a pack, but even then they are only interested in the welfare of their group and unite merely for aggression. Such species are usually ferocious.

When protection is sought against natural elements, it is obtained either by finding natural shelters like caves and holes or through individual effort by building nests or combs, as is the manner of birds and bees. In this case, there is not much predatory activity, as the creature makes its own contribution towards the creation of the needed supply.

Safety from outside attack is often obtained by the flocking or herding together of certain kinds of animals like sheep, cattle, elephants, etc. In this form there is a strong feeling of social dependence, and such animals are, generally passive and peacefull and not aggressive and ferocious like wolves. For distinction we shall call animals which unite for aggression, such as wolves, "the pack type" and those which gather together for safety "the herd type."

Mankind :

If we analyse carefully the history of man, we shall find the above types reflected in his economic activity in different stages of his evolution. The primitive savage gathered his fruits and edible herbs, clothed himself with material such as leaves and skins provided by nature and sought shelter in caves and other protected places. Next came the hunter and fisher who produced tools with which they killed or caught other forms of living creatures for their own use. The nomad, on the other hand captured animals and domesticated them and utilized their products. He wandered from place to place in search of food and fodder. At a much later stage man began to control his environment and produce natural conditions favourable for his purpose and enjoyed the fruits of his labour. When he did this he attained the agricultural stage of civilization.

As civilization advanced, the need for a greater division of labour was felt. Industrialization began in various forms according to the genius of the people in different places.

The economic organizations developed by civilized man under industrialization bear marks of these earlier type of evolution according to the stage of development from which the particular organization took its origin. Generally speaking, the animals' activities are individualistic except in the case of gregarious vegetarian animals of the "herd type" which get together for safety, or in the case of the "pack type" of carnivorous creatures, which unite for aggressive purpose in search of food. The hunter and nomad, who are essentially of the "pack type" are individualistic and predatory and do not consider the rights and privileges of other creatures.

Test of Civilization :

We must bear in mind that the true test of civilization is not our material possessions or our manner or mode of life but the thought we bestow on the well-being of others. In predation, which is really barbarism, we cannot expect to find any civilization, for true culture shifts the emphasis from "rights" to "duties". Consideration for feeling of others and a sense of responsibility towards them distinguish the "gentleman" from the boor.

When we get to the agricultural stage of civilization we find that a sense of respect for the rights of others and a feeling of one's own limited sphere of exploitation evolves with the laying out of boundaries and landmarks. From this in its turn, grows a sense of responsibility for one's own actions and their consequences on others. In this stage of civilization the economic organization is not individualistic as in the earlier stages, but becomes socialized much in the same way as the herd type of animals. Activities are controlled impersonally by means of rules of conduct and by a well conceived regulatory machine. The time taken to pass from one stage to another may be counted in thousands of years since the characteristics of the earlier stages have to be eradicated or modified and the characteristics of the next stage formed. If there is not sufficient time between one stage and another for human nature to evolve, there is a disruption or maladjustment in human society.

Characteristics :

Broadly speaking, we may classify human economic organizations into two types, the individualistic type and the social type, or, if we wish to name them clearly with reference to the animal prototype from which they originated, we may call them "the pack type" and the "herd type."

In the "pack type" are found the following characteristics :

(1) Short time outlook on life.

(2) Central control and concentration of power in the hands of individuals or small groups in a personal way.

(3) Rigorous discipline.

(4) Disregard of the welfare of the actual workers or contributors to the success of the organization.

(5) Suppression of individuality of the worker and a spirit of intolerance either in competition or in rivalry.

(6) The prospect of obtaining gains provides the motive force for all activities.

(7) Concentration of the benefits obtained and the sharing of them amongst a limited few.

(8) To gathering in as much as one can without reference to the altruistic value of service rendered, the object being predatory.

We may add that owing to the concentration of power and benefit, these activities generally radiate from a limited geographical area such as cities.

In the "herd type", on the other hand we find :

(1) Long time outlook on life.

(2) Social control, decentralization and distribution of power, the working and regulation being impersonal.

(3) Activity steered into desired channels by rules of conduct and social regulatory machinery.

(4) Attempts made to safeguard the weak and the helpless.

(5) Encouragement given to individual growth and expressed by a considerable amount of tolerance.

(6) Activities directed by a consideration of certain set ideals and social movements.

(7) Distribution of gains as wide as possible according to the needs of individuals.

(8) The object is to satisfy needs judged from an altruistic point of view.

Because of the attempt to decentralize control and production, economic activity is broad-based, being scattered over a wide geographical area in the form of village groups.

In the light of these facts, we shall attempt in the following two chapters to analyse some of the forms of economic organization evolved by the human race.

———

CHAPTER 2 WESTERN ECONOMIC ORGANIZATIONS

Although, in point of time, Western organization evolved much later than our own, we shall consider their merits and demerits first because the ostensible object of this book is to enable us to lay a foundation for the proper evolution of the future economic organization of our country.

Different Types:

Owing to the fact that Western peoples had no time to settle down to an agricultural civilization which they had only just attained when industrialization overtook them, we find a great number of points at which their economic organization dovetails into the hunter and nomad stages of evolution. Consequently, the characteristics of the "pack type" which we considered in the last chapter, stand well pronounced in their industrial organizations. We may classify them into five main groups according to the personnel of the central controlling group, and, as the masses, whether of the West or of the East, are of much the same kind, we may eliminate them.

1. The dynasty of might.
2. The dynasty of finance.
3. The dynasty of the machine.
4. The dynasty of labour.
5. The dynasty of the middle classes.

The dynasty of might is represented by the feudal organization in which the feudal baron with his retinue under military discipline descended on the villages from his castle and compelled the producing masses to surrender part of the fruits of their labour to him for no conceivable return beyond the doubtful protection afforded by him from the attacks of marauders other than himself. The return for his services or the amount rendered to him was tribute. The benefit so received was mainly for the use of the feudal baron. Any thought of the welfare of the villagers who surrendered a share of the products to the baron never occured to him. What did Napolean care how many of his soldiers he left dead on the way so long as he could get to Moscow ?

Towards the end of the 18th century we find the dynasty of finance coming into evidence with the commercial exploitation of inventions and the accumulation of capital secured through centuries of economic activities. Owing to religious persecution, men with original thinking powers sought shelter from middle Western Europe in Great Britain. At that time, Britain was a poor country and had not the requistite accumulation of capital to bring to full fruition the benifit of imported brain power. This desideratum was made possible by Empire Builders directing the flow of gold from the Ganges to the Thames. With the rise of financial power the feudal baron found it to his advantage to join hands with the financer. This combination of might and finance led to what is called in modern times "Imperialism". In this also there is need of discipline in the form of "team work" and the return that the organization gets is called "interest" as against the "tribute" of the feudal lord. The control is centralized and the success of each organization depends upon the person or persons directing the institution. The recognition of the importance of discipline in the form of joint effort for the success of the financial dynasty is evinced by the fact that "team work" is almost deified in Great Britain. Games which are based on team work such as cricket, football, hockey and boat-racing have become national sports and those who excel in these games are considered almost heroes and fit to carry on the work of the empire. In this system, too, all that mattered was the interest that the financier received. The welfare of the producer was again forgotten. Did King Leopold of Belgium think of the mutilated bodies of the natives of the Congo so long as he got his returns from their forced labour ?

America is the best example of machine civilization. There, man stood aghast at the might of nature. He had to grow artificial hands in the form of machinery to grapple with vast distances, mighty rivers and impenetrable forests in order to make them serve his needs. These circumstances led to the development of machinery as a labour saving device. By its very origin the control was limited to the few and the interests of those who contributed to the production were ignored. The factory workers might be made into minced meat but the machinery of the meat packers of Chicago could not be stopped to save the life of a labourer.

Under this dynasty, discipline took the form of a speeding process and standardization of the article. This organization also partakes of all the characteristics mentioned in the "pack-type" and the return that is obtained from the use of the machine represents the profits to the machine-owner.

When opportunity occurred, exploited labour turned the tables on the feudal barons, the financier, and the machine-owner and took its turn at the helm and thus we find communism organized in the "pack type". In this system also, most of the characteristics of the other organization are represented *viz.*, centralization of control and power, rigid discipline and suppression of the individual in regard to production and distribution. Whatever good may have been obtained or envisaged by the directing body giving primary consideration to the needs of the community and not so much to the amount of profit obtained, yet the organization too is a sectarian or class organization run by the proletariat with special privileges attached to the sect in power.

More recently, we find the struggle of the middle classes to seize power represented in organizations such as Nazism and Fascism, both based on much the same lines as capitalism.

Common Features :

All these organizations are city-centred and in time will lead to degeneration of the producing masses because no initiative is left to them, their function being merely one of carrying out higher orders. Already, within a period of one or two generations, we find in the most well-organized capitalistic country, America, the nervous diseases, due to the strain involved in the system of economic production, are giving cause for alarm. In New York State one person out of every 22 is said to be in an asylum. Ther are 81,000 feeble-minded and 40,000 insane in hospitals. About 400,000 children are so sub-normal that they are unable to follow the ordinary curricula of schools, and in the U. S. A. as a whole, there are eight times the number of feeble-minded as there are consumptives. It is said that mental diseases in America are far more dangerous than tuberculosis, cancer, heart disease, kidney troubles, typhus, plague and cholera all put together. An economic organization that leads to this situation cannot be self-propagating, in as much as any organization should be able to produce its own leaders. But all modern capitalistic methods, in so far as they lead to the degeneration of the people engaged in them, carry within themselves the seeds of their own destruction and, therefore, will cease to exist in course of time. When therefore, we seek to establish a suitable form of economic organization for our country, we cannot accept a type that leads to the production of mental defectives.

It is because of this nervous strain that the clamour for "leisure" in industrialized countries of the West is so loud. Under their system, leisure is a necessity as their organization is unnatural. Again the nervous strain calls for something to soothe the nerves. This makes the worker to resort to drink and other vices. Natural work, on the other hand, causes physical weariness for which rest and repose in sleep are sufficient recuperatives.

The working of all these organizations is lubricated by educating the masses into thinking that happiness is to be obtained by developing a multiplicity of wants. Sanctions based on violence are essential to these systems.

Conclusion :

While "pack type" organizations have their evils, they have also some strong points. We may include the first three dynasties of might, finance and machine under "Capitalism".

Under capitalism the profit motive is given free play and individuals are allowed to exploit every situation to their gain even at the cost of injuring society. The advantage of this system is that every individual gets an opportunity to exercise his talents and energy as he likes. In trying to check this, the communists have gone to the other extreme by doing away altogther with the profit motive. Under their system, a small idealistic group plans the work for the nation. Individual talent and initiative are entirely suppressed. While the individualistic outlook of capitalism is bad, it is also a mistake to suppress man to the extent of making him into an automaton incapable of thinking for himself. Both extremes have to be avoided. In one the individualistic outlook appears in an exaggerated form, in the other, the personality of the individual is utterly crushed. While the first is based on uncontrolled selfish greed, the other is based on class hatred.

We contend that both under capitalism and communism human values are not fully taken into account. Every individual has a personality which, when properly developed, has its contribution to make to society. We have no right to look upon the common run of human beings, as either gun-fodder as under capitalism, or a cogwheel in a machine as under communism. We should not wholly reject either centralization or private ownership; nor may we entirely ban the profit motive nor advocate complete decentralization. What we want to find is a mean between capitalism and communism. Both systems have failed to bring out the best in individuals, and both have led to group violence; capitalism by trying to find markets and communism by keeping out the foreigner and trying to enforce its plan. Hence, we have to modify both While we do not reject the profit motive, we shall have to try and curb the capacity of the individual to accumulate profits and wealth. We human beings are so built that progress can only be possible with the advance of each individual. For the advance of each individual, it is necessary to allow a certain amount of self-interest. This is fully demonstrated in everyday life. When a man works for a fixed salary, as say, in a Government post, the contribution he makes to society is generally of a routine nature. The greatest inventions and discoveries have been the results of venturesome spirits attempting to give expression to their inner urge. Decentralization of production ensures the producer the product of his labour. Therefore, if group production has disadvantages the alternative is decentralized production. While it may be granted that group activity has a contribution to make within a limited community, it is open to serious doubt whether such activity is possible on a national scale for any length of time. A few idealists may get together and run an Ashram or other philanthropic institutions on the basis of service but whether such principles can be applied in the present stage of varied and varying civilizations on a world basis may be questioned. For even Russia finds it necessary to shut herself out from the outside world in order to carry out communist experiments. Foreign trade is a state monopoly, and intercourse with foreign nations is highly restricted. Thus, the communistic experiment is carried on almost in a laboratory. Experiments may be carried on under controlled circumstances in order to find out the laws that govern economic movements but it is too much to expect humanity, as a whole, to function in like manner under normal conditions without such controlled environment.

Centralized production under Capitalism, with the profit motive as its propelling force, directs labour from the supply of primary needs to luxuries, from food to face powder, because the margin of profit is greater on luxury goods than on comfort supplies and the profits on the latter are greater than on the goods for primary needs. A rupee in the hands of a poor man may represent two day's food for him and his family, but the same coin in the hands of a millionaire may represent merely the value of a drink or a smoke. Therefore, the money in the hands of the poor man has a high value in commodities while the very same amount in the hands of a rich man represents little utility. Hence, any production that aims at gathering in the largest number of rupees will naturally cater for the needs of the rich man who will throw away his money with the greatest ease. It follows that luxury articles provide a larger percentage of profit for the producer, it being easier to make a profit by making lip-sticks, or such other toilet articles used by the rich, than by supplying, the needs of the poor in the shape of reed mats or mud utensils. Hence, it is that we find a world facing starvation and overproduction at the same time.

Centralized production, whether under Capitalism or under Communism, will in the long run lead to national deterioration, as there is only a limited scope for the exercise of the entrepreneur's ability. Not a little of the unbusinesslike habits of our people is due to lack of opportunity for their assuming responsibility whether in business or in Government. Unless one is allowed to strike out for oneself, there can be no healthy growth. We cannot have a nation of stalwarts on centralized methods. Both political and economic freedom need decentralization if they are to germinate. The right place for a machine is an instrument in the hands of man, but when man is turned into a machine—feeder, the whole organization is up-side-down. Man does not exist for the machine.

Under Communism, society is made a fetish of and individuals sink into insignificance. However many material comforts a person may be provided with by society, what shall it profit him if he loses his personality ?

Communistic production takes the form of military discipline in the economic sphere and too much regimentation and discipline is bad for growth. Soviet Communism is also based on class hatred. Indeed, it is an outcome of class hatred. Even today, there are distinctly marked differences in the treatment of peasants and workers. While under Imperialis violence is directed towards foreigners and strangers, th violence of Communism is internal. Its own people have t suffer it. If what we hear about the violent methods adopte to suppress the bourgeois class has even an iota of truth in it no lover of human progress can advocate such methods i any group. Because, if we sow a wind we reap a whirlwind We cannot afford to lay the foundation stone of a new orde for ourselves on class hatred.

It is argued that if we are to have any form of Govern ment, violence is essential. As has already been pointed ou a certain amount of violence will always be involved in any state control, but what matters is the degree and the spirit behind what appears to be violence. Even a loving father chastises his child. If there is violence in such chastisement, then there is bound to be such violence also in a Government as we conceive it. If the Government is truly democratic it will represent the people. In such a Government, any regulatory functions that require violence, will be self-inflicted and so it is nothing more than self-discipline.

CHAPTER 3 EASTERN ECONOMIC ORGANIZATIONS

It is in old countries such as India, China and Japan (as she was) that we find agricultural civilization influencing economic organization. Such civilizations are the results of philosophical and conscious social planning. The western systems are haphazard growths without any thought behind them. In this sense the West can hardly be said to have a civilization at all. It is more refined barbarism. The only exception in the West to this is Soviet Russia, which is the first attempt at a well-planned society in the West with a sociological philosophy, good or bad, behind it. In the oriental type, the social organization of the country is harnessed to direct and control economic activity. It is a far cry from the "pack" to the "herd" type. The countries which have worked on the latter methods have evolved social systems which are very similar to one another. In the "pack type" there is the common characteristic of aggression for economic purposes, but in this type there is a getting together not for aggression but for internal safety and consolidation. As a matter of fact, in Mongolian countries, foreigners were excluded until very recently, and in India foreign travel was looked down upon and definitely discouraged. Merchants alone went out of the country for commercial purposes. The regulation and decentralization of power made the entire organization work in an impersonal way, the driving power being obtained by hitching the economic machinery either to civil laws or to religion or superstition. The interests of the weak and the helpless were safeguarded by provisions which none could break with impunity. As a result, we find in India such institutions as the joint family system, the division of labour by caste, and the method of distribution to artisans of a share in the products of agriculture.

All the members of a joint family shared what was provided by the earning members. If one had a large income, one's brother, who was incapable of working, was also supported. The large income being shared amonsgst all the members of the family made the distribution of wealth more equitable, and uncontrolled competition, such as would have been possible for extremely wealthy individuals, was thereby curbed. The joint famly system, not only avoided competition and mal-distribution of wealth, but it also offered protection to the incapable and the weak. The caste system aimed at directing the various units of economic activity in consonance with one another and safeguarding the community from over-production through personal good and uncontrolled competition. *The puddi, dan or the baluta* system of payment in kind to the artisans assured to every individual a minimum of subsistence. The carpenter, the blacksmith and the chamar produced their articles and supplied them to the people in the villages free of money charges, taking in return, a share in the production of local agriculture which afforded there a minimum subsistence allowance. The organization itself was not one suited for the exploitation of the weak by the strong. The principles underlying these systems appear to be based on the conception that work itself is a method of distribution of wealth. The community was regarded as a corporate unit with its various members performing their own function and contributing to the life of the community, as a whole, just as the different members of our body work together, share a common life and form a unit. It would not do, for instance, for the heart to quarrel with the hands or the feet, or for the stomach to refuse nourishment to the heart. These systems also promoted solidarity and co-operation within the groups and provided little chance for exploitation. People working within such an organization were like sheep folded in a pen and sheltered from wolves in the shape of exploiters. Exploitation itself was not altogether absent, but the purpose of the organization was to minimise opportunities for such and offer protection to the innocent by putting up social barriers. These old systems are now not capable of bearing the strain put on them by the tremendous expansion in the field of economic activity. It will be necessary for us, however, to consider carefully the systems evolved under old conditions and devise ways and means of similary organizing present day production without involving a nervous strain on the producer and, at the same time, ensuring to every worker the fruits of his labour. We have seen that the "pack type" had given unbridled scope to the venturesome under its theory of *laissez faire* and its corollary of the independence of the individual, while the "herd type" recognized that the selfishness of the individual had to be curbed in the interest of society as a whole.

In Other Spheres :

When we look at the West and the East from these points of view, we notice that the distinction made between the "pack type" in the economic world is also to be observed in other spheres such as the political, religious and social. In the political field, we find true democracy absent in all Western countries. It masquerades under the cloak of parliamentary organization in which real power is vested in a group or in a single dominating personality. Similarly even in a personal and tolerant religion, such as was practised by Jesus we find, as organized in the West, concentration of authority and power in one person, the Pope, or in an institution such as the church. The outcome of this has been bigoted intolerance. In social life also we find fashions dictated from palaces slavishly followed in the cottages, and the whole structure of society taking its cue from the cities. The civilization that has developed has been a city civilization originating from Greece and Rome.

In India, on the other hand, in the political field in the past, village republics managed their own affairs. Even when foreign invaders came, the everyday life of the villager was left undisturbed. In religion we notice the same tendency to decentralize the form of worship and views in regard to the Godhead, with the result that there was extreme tolerance. In social life grandeur was centred in the palace and the temple, while the life of the children was generally simple and suited to village conditions. The people's desire for pageantry and colour found artistic outlets in festivals connected with the palace and the temple, leaving no room for personal display.

Thus, we make the fundamental difference between the "pack" and the "herd" types. India has been under the "herd type" for centuries and has evolved a culture, which cannot support without detriment to itself, the superstructure of the "pack type". We constantly notice the difficulty that is felt in India in getting a small body of men to work without questioning the authority of the leader, which is the simplest of the requirements of the "pack type". A causal scrutiny of any newspaper will show the difficulties that bodies such as District Boards find in pulling together. There is a fundamental reason for this which has its roots in the civilization that has evolved through centuries in our country. We shall have to note these variations in formulating a system of economic production best suited to modern conditions and capable of working satisfactorily in India, if industrialization is not to bring with it all the evils attendant on its development in the West.

If we attempt to superimpose a foreign structure on our ancient foundation, the edifice will certainly tumble like a pack of cards. A plant that flourishes in Russia under hot-house conditions may not thrive if transplanted in our country. The "pack type" is short-sighted and selfish and its control is centralized, and personal, when, however, the control is socialized and decentralized, the policy can be a long-sighted one.

The following table gives a broad outline indicating the origin of the various systems considered in this and the preceding chapters.

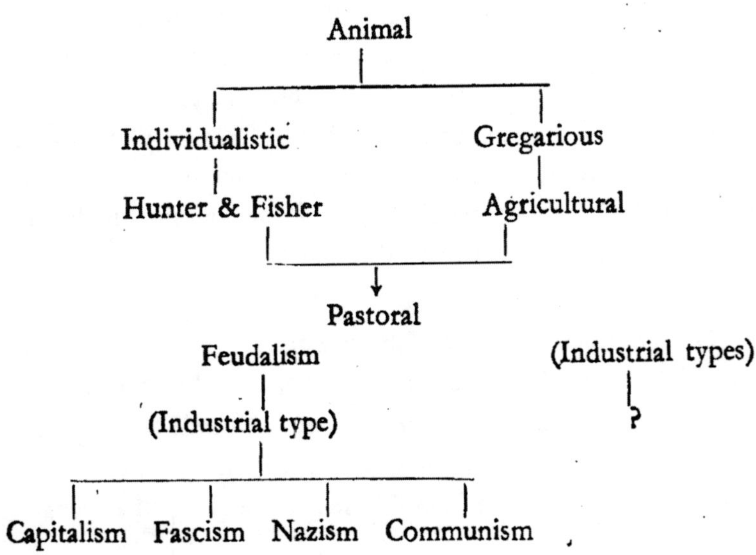

The West has evolved some systems based on its own "pack type" civilization for its industrial life. India had an agricultural "herd type" civilization which is now decadent.

The Four Castes :

We have fallen away from our ideals, and if we are to rebuild again, we have to regain the principles that guided our forefathers. Our degeneration is largely due to deterioration in our national character and to selfishness in individuals. Society consists of a variety of people. We can classify them in four groups. (1) The idealistic : Those who take a long range view of life and live their lives in ideals. (2) The altruistic : Those whose range of view is comparatively limited but is still beyond their own span of life. (3) The materialistic : Those whose vision is limited to their own lives. (4) Those who follow in a rut without much imagination. In the Varanashram these are called respectively the Brahmin, the Kshatriya, the Vaisya and the Sudra.

The Brahmin is one who sees far into the future. He therefore, forgets his mud shell of a body and lives in his ideals. His symbol is the beggar's bowl. He will sacrifice his all to attain his ideal. He knows no compromises. This must be the lot of all brain workers. They are sterilized economically from mis-appropriating the fruits of their natural endowments for their selfish ends. Their purpose in life is the service of the community through pure means, and their reward is status and honour.

On the other hand, the Kshatriya though he also sees far enough to count his body as nothing, yet he will not go further than the society in which he lives. He will be prepared to compromise to that extent where it will help society. His symbol is the flag. He loses himself in seeking the welfare of society. His glory is the service of his fellowmen and his reward is position and power.

The third type is circumscribed by his skin. He cannot see any further. His ideals are limited to his escaping the jail and making the best of life. He is self-centred and his symbol is the balance. This is the Vaisya, the materialistic merchant and entrepreneur, who amasses wealth but gets no social honour or position other than what he may secure by dedicating his possessions for the use of the community.

Then we see the Sudra with not even the venturesomeness and imagination of the Vaisya. He prefers a well laid outline. He is happy with his salary, pension and provident fund.

For example an electrician who lives to explore the possibilities of the science without any regard to personal gain is a Brahmin. One who learns the science with the object of helping to industrialize his country and thereby rainse the economic standards of his people is a Kshatriya. He who takes contracts or deals in electric supply or goods in consideration of material gain is a Vaishya. But the man who wants to enter the Government electrical department because of the permanency of tenure, economic security and a pension is a Sudra.

A Brahmin by birth, who practises law to make money exploiting the quarrelsomeness of human nature, is a Bania and not a Brahmin. A Kshatriya by birth who accepts office under a foreign Government is no true Kshatriya as he sells himself into slavery for money. A Kshatriya worthy of his salt will give his blood for freedom and not barter away his soul.

Pruned of all extraneous growth, this is the core of the caste system. It curbs devastating cut-throat competition as a factor in social alignment and emphasises co-operation and obedience as the basis of all law and order. It is graded on a cultural standard of values almost unknown to money economy. Material considerations sink into insignificance when human needs claim our attention. Duty and not out rights determines our position in society. Once these conditions are firmly established we shall have prepared the way of peace when war shall be no more.

CHAPTER 4 SCHOOLS OF ECONOMICS

Types of Natural Resources :

We may divide the supply of materials into two types; those in limited and fixed supply such as minerals, coal, petroleum etc. and those that can be increased by man's effort or are inexhaustible, such as timber, cotton, water etc. The former may be termed the "Reservoir Economy" and the latter "Current Economy".

The Reservoir Economy is the easier of the two economies and produces quick results but as it gets exhausted it leads to violence.

The Current Economy, though it needs a good deal of man's effort to maintain and is slower in responding, yet it does not promote violence.

To illustrate these forms we shall look at the lives of each of two sons of a father who bequeaths to each rupees ten thousand. The first son takes his share, goes to a nearby town and lives a luxurious life on it. He runs through the capital in a little time but has acquired a taste for luxurious life. He will turn to doubtful ways of making money by gambling, cheating etc.

The second son invests his share in business and lives on the profit it brings say Rs. 150/- per month. He need not have recourse to bad ways to maintain himself.

The first—reservoir economy—may give a flashy and glamorous life but will lead to destruction, while the second—

current economy—needs self-control, is simple but self-respecting and does not encroach on other lives.

Schools of Economics :

The various forms of human activities that we have examined so far can be classified, according to the predominant motive force that shapes them, into four characteristic schools.

1. Economy of Predation
2. Economy of Enterprise
3. Economy of Gregarianism
4. Economy of Permanence

ECONOMY OF PREDATION

As we have already noted the simplest form of satisfying one's needs is to help oneself to an existing supply without having contributed anything to bring that supply into existence. Hunting, fishing and, to a large extent, quarrying and exploitation of minerals will fall under this category. The activating principle is one 's own need irrespective of any rights or duties or any other consideration. This is of the lowest type and if one can apply economics to the animal kingdom we shall find that the activities of animals fall within this method of action. This method leads to life on an animal plane where one desires to obtain something for nothing.

ECONOMY OF ENTERPRISE

The next stage is one of exercising the rights of the individual. A person is endowed with certain talents and he uses it for his own benefit and jealously seeks to keep out anyone else benefiting from it or interfering with his line of activity. This is the most elementary human stage. Man creates a supply and holds it for himself. The outcome of this stage is the *laissez-faire* attitude to all Government control and the capitalistic mentality. Europe and America have been labouring for the most part of the last century under the grip of this self-centred attitude to life. Every man to himself and devil take the hindermost is the ruling motto. This is the high road to self-indulgence and gratification and is mostly unitary and individualistic.

ECONOMY OF GREGARIANISM

As man becomes more and more conscious that no one lives unto himself but that there are certain ties that bind man and man he develops a gregarious attitude. Even here there are certain grades of recognition given to associates.

(a) Imperialism :

The most elementary of these leads to a combination amongst those of a homogeneous group held together by selfish interest as in cartels, combines, trusts, and monopolies. This group with an overdose of the Economy of Predation leads to Imperialism where one group contrives to exploit the labour and resources of another for its own benefit. Here again the principle of self-interest controls all activity which is based on one's own rights regardless of one's duties. This emphasises group interests to the exclusion of all other considerations.

(b) Fascism, Nazism, Communism & Socialism :

Where a heterogeneous groups of a type, ethnical, social, economic etc. have common ideals, interests or ends they combine for their own benefit or the achievement of their common goal. Here there is a slight recognition of one's duties, but it is limited to those of the same group, and there is a predominant self-centred group interest as opposed to those outside the group. This form has led to various orders of society being inaugurated during this century. They have taken slighty differing courses but the underlying factors are much the same. There is less of predation in this than under Imperialism as the group is generally wider but it leads to intense nationalism. The higher cultural values are forgotten and man is to live by bread alone. The underlying duties of one group towards another find little place in their scheme for the world.

THE ECONOMY OF PERMANENCE

All the forms of economies we have seen so far may be grouped as the Economies of Transience because they are all based on the fleeting interests that govern the short span of an individual's life or even that of a group or nation. If we aim at permanence we must found our actions on eternal principles.

When we emphasise mainly rights, life will lead to indulgence, while considerations of duties will lead to an evaluation of each life in terms of the lives of the others, and, therefore, will make for permanence. Man is a piece of the Divine seeking his ultimate union with the Infinite through the love of life all around him. His end is not self-indulgence and enjoyment during his short span of three score years and ten. He should look at himself in the perspective of eternity and exclaim : "What is man that Thou are mindful of him ?" We have no continuing city here. We are all camp-dwellers and sojourners.

It is through such a belief in the Divine ordering of the universe that Gandhiji holds that the upheavals that mar the even course of human history are the outcome of man's sin in so far as he deviates from the Divine Will. As long as man follows this Divine order there can be but duties to guide his actions towards his fellowmen-Dharma in the course for all things permanent.

Principles of Economics tend to be permanent in the measure in which we recognise the transience of life and formulate our laws in perspective of eternity. Such an attitude alone will lead to the progress and prosperity of the human race and to a life of peace and goodwill based on culture and refinement. Hence we need to study this science from objective standards and approach the application of it in relation to laws that govern the universe and not measure it by man's needs of the moment.

In an order so conceived we have to be sparing in exploiting natural resources and must base it on the consumption of labour and of materials that can be created by man which can be available always, rather than live by predation by drawing on natural reservoirs. They lays the emphasis of distribution. Such an organization will give expression to a mode of life very different from what is considered "modern" in the West. Iron will be used sparigngly as mines are reservoirs which will be exhausted in time. As far as possible all our requirements must come from things that can be produced by man. The supply of wood can be increased by carefully planning the growth and administration of forests. The "modern" world is of Iron and Steel. We cannot afford to draw on our inheritance too freely and extravagantly. Brick and mortar, cement and wood belong to the regime of the Economy of Permanence while reinforced concrete buildings, steel doors and cabinets are of the transient order. Strange as it may seem the mud-huts of India belong to the Economy of Permanence while the steel and concrete sky scrapers of

New York are symbols of the Economy of Transience. Similarly, in all other departments of life man has to rely more on his own efforts than the apparent abundance of nature to supply his needs. This will give a fresh orientation to our standards of life.

The recognition of the fact that material things are impermanent and that the grave is not our goal drives us to evaluate affairs of a nation on the basis of permanent values. We find an effort at such organization in the old Hindu order of Society. While in the predatory European Society the first place is granted to the forces which are essential to its existence—Army and Navy—(in Great Britain because of its insular position the Navy comes first in status), Hindu Society was graded according to the pursuit of ideals.

First : The idealist who seeks to serve with pure means without personal ends—*The Brahmin.*

Second : The altruist who seeks to serve by all means without personal ends—*The Kshatriya.*

Third : The materialist who may serve but with an eye to personal gain—*The Vaishya.*

Fourth : The one who lives on the animal plane—*The Sudra.*

In an organization of this type profit cannot provide the main motive force nor can the mechanism of prices control the market. The emphasis should be on distribution and human values rather than on accumulation and money values. The goal will not be the advancement of an individual, nor even of a group or nation but that of humanity itself.

If we may classify the different economic types according to the caste nomenclature we may say that Economy of Predation is the *Sudra* type where one avoids any exertion and is content to have his wants satisfied from existing stock. Primitive and nomadic tribes follow this.

Economy of Enterprise and Imperialism belong to the *Vaishya* group. Both are to an extent predatory but they are characterized by keen ambition and willingness to put forth the best effort possible for selfish and materialistic ends. Capitalism and British Imperialism are examples of this comparatively primitive type of evolution characteristic of individuals and classes.

Economy of Gregarianism is the economics of the *Kshatriya*. It is not individualistic but it is characterized by a racial or national self-centred idealism. We may cite Nazism and Communism as good examples where individual interests are sacrificed on the altar of altruism.

Economy of Permanence is *Brahmanical* in its idealism and conception. It is an attempt to get into alignment with the order that prevails in the universe and work in unison and in tune with the Infinite. It is the highest evolution man is capable of. It is only in an order of this conception that the interests of the meanest individual will be safeguarded and the meekest unit can develop to the fullest capacity guaranteeing the onward march of humanity. We have to realise that unless steps are taken with an eye to the ultimate progress of the whole human race we are prone to be visited by lapses into barbarism which will wipe out all civilization. Planning with the principles of eternal values calls for insight and cultural advancement. It does not promise any rapid results and we have to hold our souls in patience for the mills of God work slowly. It is the way of truth and non-violence. Its rewards are moderate. But it is the only path to true democracy in political life, and to peace amongst nations.

PART II
THE MODERN SITUATION

CHAPTER 5 PEOPLE'S INCOME

[This chapter is part of the author's contribution to the Oxford Pamphlet on Indian Affairs-Economic Background and is reproduced by kind permission of the Oxford University Press.]

Many attempts have been made to measure the national income, and from that to arrive at the per capita income and then to compare the results obtained in other countries by a similar process. The latest estimate of national inome of British India is by Professor V. K. R. V. Rao. His computation of the per capita income is Rs. 62 per annum. However useful such calculations may be for certain academic purposes, the picture of conditions they unveil is thoroughly misleading as regards the real circumstances prevailing in rural parts. Naturally the handicaps under which such calculations are made are many. The security and unreliability of statistics available, the lack of uniformity of treatment, the vast range over which the average is struck etc., vitiate the conclusions to which one may be led by relying too much on such figures. A theoretical calculation of this type brings the income to about Rs. 5/- a month. Even such an income is far too low to ensure a satisfactory balanced diet on a subsistence level, not to mention provision for clothing and shelter.

A more reliable and closer approximation to facts may be obtained by a survey of actual incomes in villages. An average struck from figures collected from over 50 villages of Matar Taluka by the present writer gives an income per capita of

Rs. 14/- per annum.* This taluka is in a comparatively prosperous part of Gujerat which province itself is better-off than many other provinces of India.

Another way of getting a more accurate picture of the income in agricultural communities is derived from the land direct, and does not figure in terms of money. A calculation based on a survey of over 600 villages of the Central Provinces discloses a per capita income of Rs. 12/- per annum.† This amount will not cover even half the cost of a low subsistence diet. Therefore, even assuming that all the income is used for obtaining food, the people have to remain half-fed at best.

WHY IS IT SO LOW ?

Granting that the standard of living is below the subsistence level, we have to probe deeper to ascertain the reasons. It is wrong to attribute low standards in India to the inculcation of ascetic ideals. People go half-starved, not because they desire to be slim but because they cannot get enough to eat. They have no purchasing power to make their demand effective. When the people are industrious and intelligent it is no argument to say that they are inefficient. We have to look elsewhere for satisfactory reasons to explain why their productivity should be so low.

A person may be willing to work hard and may be intelligent but may have no opportunity to occupy himself gainfully, or if he does have employment it may not bring inadequate return for his labours. The standard of living of an individual under such conditions is bound to be low due to no fault of his. This appears to be the position in our country.

* Survey of Matar, Taluka, P. 70.

† C. P. Goverment Industrial Survey Committee Report Part I.

LACK OF OPPORTUNITIES

Even a cursory glance through the list of imports and exports will reveal the fact that the bulk of our imports are manufactured goods, and the exports are largely raw materials. The process of transforming a raw material into a manufactured article involves employment for the people. When we export raw materials we are creating unemployment for our people by depriving them of the opportunities of work. At the same time when we import finished goods, we employ foreign labour to the exclusion of our own. Applying this reasoning, our foreign trade is an open record of the transfer of our opportunities of employment to foreign countries.

How this is directed is a long story. No protection was afforded to struggling infant industries. Railway freight rates are designed so as to encourage the shipment of raw materials from the ports and the transport of finished goods to the interior. Heavy taxes and dues at the source of raw materials, a bad policy in regard to communications, the building of roads and canals, etc., have discouraged the growth of industries. Hardly any research calculated to help the villager's production has been carried on. Government expenditures have not patronised local production and have set wrong standards of efficiency, leading to large supplies for Government departments being obtained from foreign countries. The educational system was not calculated to help young men to enter industries and commerce as entrepreneurs. It will not be possible within the space at our disposal to go into the details of these false steps, but the above enumeration indicates to the reader the methods which have deprived the people of their birthright. Added to these are the uncertainties of a countryside dependent on the vagaries of the monsoon for its agricultural operations. These fortuitous circumstances have produced the unemployment and underemployment of the people, thus lowering their income.

UNREMUNERATIVE STAGES

The return that a manufacturer obtains at the various stages in the course of processing the raw material into the finished product varies. In the earlier stages—near the raw material—the return is small, and as the article reaches the consumption stage the gain increases. If all these stages take place in one and the same country, the income of the country, as a whole, will not be affected. The distribution of wealth may not be uniform, but will adjust and level itself in time. If on the other hand, these various stages are so separated by political boundaries that the badly-paying earlier stages are in one country and the more remunerative later stages are in another country, without the possibility of settling down to a common level, then we have watertight comparmenpts in which the country undertaking the earlier process of manufacture has to be content with a lower income than the country where the finished goods are produced.

For instance, let us examine a chain of producers working on the basis of cottage units, manufacturing hair-oil from groundnuts. If a farmer with about four acres of cultivable land, which is more than an average holding in India, produces Rs. 100 worth of groundnuts at a cost of Rs. 70/- for seeds and land operations, taking five months for the crop, the farmer's income will be Rs. 30/-. If he is fortunate enough to raise anther crop during the year of wheat he will have a net income of say Rs. 50/- from it. These gains, totalling Rs. 80/-, will represent his annual income.

If an oil-presser takes these Rs. 100/- worth of groundnuts and presses out oil, the operation will take him about a month during which period the upkeep of his bullock will cost Rs. 10/-

and he will obtain as a product Rs. 125/- worth of oil and Rs. 25/- worth of oil-cake. Thus, he gets an inome of Rs. 40/- per month. Where adequate finances are forthcoming to enable the oil presser to stock sufficient groundnuts for crushing during the whole year he can secure an income of Rs. 500/- per year at this rate.

The hair-oil manufacturer can convert this Rs. 125/- worth of groundnut oil into scented hair-oil, at the cost of Rs. 245/- for deodorizing, scenting and bottling, in about a month, yielding Rs. 500/- worth of such scented oil. This will give him an income of Rs. 130/- per month, and with the necessary capital he can get employment throughout the year, getting an income of about Rs. 1,500/- annually.

The facts stated above show that owing to the vagaries of the monsoon and the nature of his calling the farmer gets only Rs. 80/- per year, while the oil-presser, if he can command sufficient finances, can manage to occupy himself throughout the year and obtain an income of Rs. 500/- per year; similarly, the manufacturer of hair-oils may gain Rs. 1,500/- per year. We notice that as the process comes nearer the consumption stage more capital but less personal labour is needed. This aspect will be even more accentuated if centralized methods are resorted to. As it is, to keep one hair-oil manufacturer engaged right through the year we need about a dozen farmers on the verge of starvation to supply the requisite oil-seeds. Even then, if all were in the same country, in course of time the varying incomes would adjust themselves within a limited range. But if the farmers were in India and the manufacturers in Germany this variation in the income of the different groups would never have the opportunity of readjustment but would lead to increasing divergence rasulting in progressive poverty in the former country and accumulated riches in the latter—the raw material producers being assigned in perpetuity to low-income-yielding occupations and the manufacturing ruling nations reserving to themselves the more profitable avocations. Thus we see the reasons for the competition amongst the nations to be the ruling race, and to hold others in bondage as the raw material producers for themselves. This is the basis of all imperialism, which consigns the less remunerative task of producing raw materials to the subject races, and reserves the more remunerative functions to the rulers. This method of dividing the functions between nations is bound to consign the raw material producing nations to an economic state of progressively increasing poverty which will ultimately result in the deterioration of the culture of those nations. In the course of the last century, with the growth of industrialization in Europe and America, India has slowly slipped into this lower order. Hence the low share she is getting out of the great wealth the human race is pouring out today. The problem is not one of production but one of a fair method of distributing the gains obtained.

CHANGE IN DEMAND

India is a country abounding in labour-wealth. The people will only find a market for exchange of their wealth when articles of consumption, whose main costs are labour costs, are in demand. With the growth of mechanized industries in the West and a drive towards labour-saving devices, the market was flooded with goods in which the labour cost was very low, the major part of the cost being for raw materials, transport, insurance, marketing and overhead charges. Thus the capitalists established themselves in the markets everywhere, while labour was ousted. In India, with a scarcity of capital and abundance of labour, this situation intensified unemployment and underemployment, when even such labour cost as entered into the cost of the manufactured article came largely from foreign lands. The only wealth of the masses in India is labour. The market for this labour has been much restricted by the advent of the products of centralized industries in the world markets and the cultivation of a philosophy of multiplicity of wants by the well-directed propaganda of vested interests. In India the satisfaction of wants so created has been directed towards goods imported from abroad by political control. In the absence of a market for the labour wealth of India the purchasing power of the masses has fallen low.

MONEY AND CREDIT ECONOMY

Our country has large internal market for all kinds of goods. If this market had been properly husbanded and directed the people would have had a never-failing demand for their products. In the last century, the growth of money economy with its monster-child 'Credit' spread its tentacles so far and wide that our internal market has been totally disorganized and captured by foreign interests. For transferring purchasing power, money and credit are unsurpassed. An honest exchange does not consist in such transfers of material values only, but should also include transfers of human and moral values. These last two are not represented in a money transaction. The bargaining power of a seller of perishable bananas or fish is not on a par with that of the buyer, the holder of imperishable gold. The growth of money-exchange has smothered all considerations of equity and justice. As long as the buyer pays the price, nothing further need be said about the transaction. Under these conditions commerce can extend its markets to the uttermost corners of the world, but cannot guarantee an equitable distribution of wealth and values. This unrestricted extension has resulted in the export of raw materials to distant industrial countries and imports of manufactured articles from such far off manufacturers with the consequent intensification of unremunerative production to our own land, noticed in an earlier paragraph.

The old Indian system of distribution was a combination of money and barter exchange, where human considerations had a place. Certain artisans, like the carpenter and blacksmith, and menials, like the barber, and the sweeper, were guaranteed their subsistence by payment in kind at the time of harvest in consideration for certain basic services to the community. This system, known as *baluta or puddi or dan*, is fast disappearing, leaving the former beneficiaries to starve out of existence in the competitive struggle of everyday life.

THE TENDENCY

Even if the income of the people was low, it would not be a matter for anxiety if the tendency over a long period was showing a steady rise. To be able to observe the tendency we have no adequate statistics prepared at periodical intervals on the same basis and principles. In the absence of such information we are, therefore, thrown back on the common-sense method of proving it. This method is perhaps the most reliable. An increase in the number of millionaries does not necessarily prove the country's prosperity. About 90 per cent of the population lives in villages, and so our enquiry should be directed towards assessing their financial conditions in the past and the present, by actual examination of their assets and social customs. Such a change in their state is well reflected in (a) their houses, (b) their hoarding of gold or investment in ornaments and (c) the carry over from their old customs.

THE EVIDENCE OF

(a) Houses and Buildings :

Any observer who comes to take stock of the state of the dwelling houses, public buildings, etc., in the villages will not be long before he notices that most of the substantial buildings are old ones, in bad repair, and that there are hardly any new ones of that ostentatious and ornate type. This reveals that the people were well-off forty or fifty years ago to be able to spend money on such buildings; while the descendents of those very same people are content to live in the dilapidated ruins of the dwellings their forefathers had erected. The financial state of the present generation does not allow of even a sufficient margin to keep these buildings in repair.

There are few public buildings, such as dharamshalas, choultries, temples, tanks and schools which are of recent origin. People have not had the wherewithal to donate such gifts. This is an unmistakable record of the weakening of the financial resources of the people.

(b) Ornaments :

Whatever the habits of the urban people in regard to commercial investments may be, the Savings Bank of the rural population will remain the hoarding of gold, or investments in ornaments. Today the village goldsmith is a rarity. Such as still exist sit before the dead embers of their smithy fires to tell a tale of woe as to how within their lifetime they have lost their profession. The fall in the prosperity of the goldsmith is an indicator of the decreased margins of savings amongst the people.

(c) Social Customs :

A customary wail against the budget of the villager is that the expenses on social occasions are excessive. No doubt this is true if we take their present scale of income as the norm. The high proportion of social expenses is itself a proof that their income, which was high enough at one time to allow of such expenditures, has now dwindled, making the ratios betwen the various items on the budget unreasonable. If a man's income is Rs. 1,000/- per annum, and he spends Rs. 100/- on marriages, etc. nobody need take up the cudgels to be labour him for extravagance. When the income of the son of such a well-to-do person falls to Rs. 300/- per annum, and he still continues, to spend the same amount of Rs. 100/- on social occasions, he will certainly be open to charges of extravagance. Social customs the world over are very tenacious. People in all lands, even though willing to forego items on the menu, will cling on to the standards of social expenditures set up by their forefathers. The lag of this item in adjusting itself to decreasing income has created this so-often-criticized disproportion, and provides valuable evidence that the income of the villagers is steadily falling.

The above three items present an indelible record written with the miseries of a people whose income has shrunk from opulence to poverty below the subsistence level.

COMPETITION WITH THE BEASTS OF BURDEN

Apart from these long-term evidences we notice that there is a growing tendency for men to compete for the work hitherto done by animals, so that they may earn a meal some-how. Bullock-drawn vehicles are now being replaced by man-power, and horse-tongas by rickshaws. Can these be the signs of prosperity ? Indeed the masses have sunk to dire poverty where they 'would fain fill their bellies with the husks that the swine did eat'.

We cannot be blindfolded by the seeming prosperity evidenced by new buildings rapidly rising in suburban areas, nor by the increase in the capital drawn from Indians for working a few industrial concerns, nor by the luxurious lives of city dwellers. India lives in the villages, and the evidence as to the prosperity or poverty of India has to be sought in the villages.

VESTED INTERESTS

One of the subsidiary sources of income of a villager used to be from carting. During the off season when their bullocks are free from farm operations and irrigation the farmers used to transport goods. With the advent of the railway and the motor lorry this source has been cut off. One can understand fish and fruits being transported by the fleeter vehicles where time is of the essence of transport, but why the lorry for transporting from forests timber, which needs time to season ? The petrol and automobile interests are too strong to be ignored. Thus every possible channel of earning an income is closing on the villagers leaving them to poverty, misery and desperation.

CHAPTER 6 NATURAL ORDER

Historically, if we follow the natural order of things, demand, as represented by hunger and by the need for shelter and protection, precedes supply (food, clothing and housing). Wherever there is a demand, a suitable supply follows—"Necessity is the mother of invention". To a certain extent, the existing demand may also be the urging factor for anticipating future wants as in the case of storing provisions against a rainy day. Compare, for example, the habits of creatures such as ants, bees, etc. in this regard.

In the case of an agricultural civilization the system ordained by nature is not interfered with to any great extent. If there is a variation at all, it follows a natural mutation. The agriculturist only aids nature or intensifies in a short time what takes place in nature in a long period. He has improved the wild varieties found in nature. He has converted grass seeds into wheat and rice by accelerating natural conditions. Similarly in economic organization, agricultural civilization has followed nature largely in the methods adopted for producing commercial products. Commodities are brought into existence either to order or to meet the usual and easily determinable market demand. A social regulating machine aids distribution, but production follows individual affort. There is no central planning unless it be to co-ordinate effort but it is not employed to set the pace. The result is that marketing functions do not create any disruption in production as the primary needs of the locality are considered first. Cities and towns merely perfom the function of distributing agents and wealth remains in the villages. Though the individual amount of wealth is comparatively small, distribution is more equable in the "pack type" where production followed that sphere where large profit could be made and thus becoming more and more centralized, led to the concentration of inordinate wealth in the hands of a few.

Under the economic system of the "pack type" derived as it is from the primitive hunter and feudal baron, we find that the variations from nature are very violent in that a large supply of goods is produced irrespective of demand and then a demand is artificially created for goods by means of clever advertisements, as for example in the case of soaps, hair-growers, tea, tonics etc. As it is to-day, the feast is spread, but there is no appetite and we have to create it by appetisers. We shall, as a consequence, suffer from indigestion as the hunger is artificial. This policy mars the even course of economic production, and leads to over-production, mal-adjustment and mal-distribution of wealth, for the whole system works from the point of view of the individual controller.

Under capitalism, the tools used are expensive. This entails a heavy overhead cost. To lessen the proportion of this expenditure the producer manufactures standardised articles on a large scale, and comes into keen competition with other producers, for the person who gets his goods into the market first gets the best of it. This leads to a glut in the market and in order to create an artificial demand, high pressure salesmanship is resorted to by means of advertisements etc. Here then the urge that brings the supply into existence is not the demand but the unnatural overhead load. This being an artificial system needs violence to make it work.

Owing to the heavy investment, a large proportion of the selling price has to be reserved for replacement, profits and interest, and only a small percentage goes to distribute purchasing power as wages. Indeed, the effort of the capitalists is directed towards reducing wages. This leads to a curtailment of purchasing power among the masses and thus limits their power to consume. Hence we witness under-consumption or relative overproduction and consequent economic depression. When there is such a congestion, war becomes a necessity to let out blood and start over again.

Under communism also the urge to produce goods is from outside the producer and, therefore, not a natural one. Hence, that too requires artificial stimulants in one form of violence or the other to sustain it.

In order to produce a better percentage of profit, producers sometimes unite and form what are called "trusts", "cartels" or "combines". While these are not wholly individualistic, they can in nowise be said to be in the interests of the nation, for they merely enlarge the circle of control and direction and continue to concentrate power and wealth. Where private motive proves to be inimical to production, socialisation of control takes place by assigning the function of direction and authority to the state. This is a variation which works satisfactorily to a limited extent in the case of public utility services, such as water supply, management of forests, and provision of communications like telephones, telegraphs, roads etc.

Barriers cause Himsa :

In regard to production, even where the regulatory functions under this "pack type" are assigned to Government, various forms of economic barriers are put up by way of control of currency and prices, fixing of freight rates and raising of tariff walls. Even Governments which work with the "pack type" usually become subject to the control of its economic organization and function for the benefit of the few who control production. In other words, in practice, under the "pack type" Governments have become mere cog-wheels in the economic machinery. There is hardly a single Government in the West that can be pointed to as being a thing apart, performing its duties purely with a view to the betterment of the masses. Not only in Capitalism but also in Communism, the state has become the main spring of the economic machinery. While the ideal is that Governments should provide the fulcrum for economic activity they have become the levers themselves with the result that the world has been turned into multifarious economic units, divided by fences which are political, geographical and ethnical.

In such a world of conflicting interests, there is litte likelihood of peaceful production, as raw materials, partly manufactured goods and finished products have perpetually to cross these artificial barriers. The greater the number of artificial barriers introduced into the flow of economic goods, the harder it becomes to keep that flow smooth and easy. Today, therefore, the world is made up of alternating stagnant pools and rapids created by these disturbing factors in the stream of economic production.

Misdirection :

Production itself does not attempt to cater for the needs of the common people but, as we have already noticed, follows activities which result in the largest profit. It is partly because of this misdirection of energy due to the profit motive that we find over-production side by side with starvation in the world today.

Under the "herd" system, as seen in India, the production of necessities was distributed in small local groups by social regulation of caste.

Under the natural order, it is essential that there should be fluidity in production and exchange. This is provided in the "herd type", as we have just seen, by the organization dividing its production centres into small units and making payments largely in kind rather than in money. The *chamar* makes the shoe and in effect exchanges it for food. The rice producer gets his shoe and gives a part of his production to the *chamar*. This completes the cycle. If, on the other hand, the rice producer buys a Japanese shoe, he cuts the ground from under his own feet, for, the village shoe-maker is to that extent impoverished and unemployed and so is unable to buy the rice producer's product, while the chances of the Japanese producer buying the rice from the buyer of the shoe are very remote. The greater probability is that the Japanese shoe manufacturer will exchange his purchasing power for obtaining his raw materials from other foreign countries, and if there were no economic friction, the money might, by taking a circuitous course, return to the rice producer in India. But as things are today, there are so many economic barriers between the Japanese shoe manufacturer and our rice producer, that the purchasing power, for all intents and purposes, never returns to the rice producer in India. Such an out-going with no return constitutes a considerable national loss of wealth

Money Economy :

Money, which was primarily introduced as a convenient medium of exchanging goods, has now come into its own under the "pack type". The whole of the capitalistic structure is based on it. It has assumed the role of a standard of values. People are educated to judge affairs on a price basis. A market value is placed even on cultural education. "Buy in the cheapest market and sell in the dearest" has become a rule of life. All other standards—aesthetic, human and altruistic—are forgotten. Thus, the golden calf has been installed on a high pedestal and the world is told to bow down before Mammon. This is a mechanical allegiance to metal. But "man does not live by bread alone". There are other things that matter which have their roots deep down in human nature. Unless our economic order is built on these natural foundations, hoarded gold will only hasten the sinking of the drowning man to the bottom of the sea.

At present, in India, our freight rates are such that the natural course of marketing is disturbed. One would imagine that Nasik grapes would sell cheaper at the Nasik railway station than Australian grapes, but owing to artificial barriers introduced in the form of freight rates, it is cheaper to buy Australian grapes in Nasik. Several similar instances might be quoted to illustrate what is meant. As long as a free flow of goods does not exist, it is folly for any one to enter distant or international markets. There is a great deal said at the present time about developing agriculture. If by this is meant that we should produce food and necessities for our millions, it will certainly be a step in the right direction, but if the aim is to produce commodities for international markets, our agriculturists will do well to beware. Already, owing to greed, our farmers have burnt their fingers by trying commercial crops during a boom season, but the same have left them in the lurch during periods of depression. They forget that they do not possess the economic reserve to step into speculative business with impunity. It will be time for us to consider production for international markets when exchange policies and prices of international markets are controlled for the benefit of all and not merely in the interests of a few who are powerful enough to make their voices heard. In the absence of such conditions, the only wise course for us is to cater for local needs and steer clear as far as possible of middlemen.

POLITICAL REACTION

As we had long been taught to look at economies through the window of money economy, most of us associate capitalism with a method of production in which accumulated wealth is sunk in the equipment needed to produce goods. This description is partly correct. If this were all, capitalism would have died long ago as there is no means of propagating itself. For the continuity of its existence capitalism has to create a clientele for itself by setting up social customs and fashions which people will follow without questioning their rationale. The life of any organization depends on its capacity thus to make a place for itself. Therefore, a more correct classification would be the one which sorts out the methods of production according to the manner by which a system seeks to control the environment and circumstances of human being so as to justify its existence and to create and retain its market and custom. Such a classification will be human rather than monetary.

AN ENSLAVING SYSTEM

The shop-keeper would like to see the wants of the people increase, he would like to supply their needs himself, and the more helpless the people are to help themselves the better will his own business be. Therefore, his interest is identical with making his customers depend on him. To this end he will study their needs most minutely and attempt to supply them better than they themselves can. The ultimate result of this will be the customer will become emaciated, numbed and paralysed for lack of scope to develop his faculties and the shop-keeper will become fat, flourishing and resourceful.

This is what is happening under centralized methods of production. We witness the degradation of races and nations who have become dependent politically and economically on those who supply their wants under various masks of trusteeship for civilizing backward races. They give their victims an opiate that with the aid of factory production people can raise their standard of living, can buy standardised goods cheaply and have more of them. In the measure in which manufacturers succeed in doping their victims into thinking that it is to the customer's advantage to take their help to that extent only can the manufacturers thrie.

We see such helplessness taking alarming strides in countries like the U.S.A. where a woman need not even cook her food. Everything is done for her. She can walk into a shop and get her soup tablets, meat and fish courses prepared and tinned, freshly made pudding and sweets, and well preserved fruits. All the trouble she needs to take is to set the table and dine. We find this trend in our country. Quaker oats, shreaded wheat, corn flakes, jams, marmalade and hundred and one things are becoming more and more common, and half-baked medical men advocate these to ill-educated women and repeat the salesman's slogans about these food articles being richer in nutrition than home made wheet *dhaliya*, seasonal fruits, etc. If this goes on, in a few years we may find our bazar stocked with *chapaties*, cooked *dal* and rice made in England and sent out in attractive containers and our ambitious medical men may tell us that these very articles prepared in the English climate and latitude have special food values as compared with food made in India ! Women, who have more money than sense, will patronise them. In time the art of cooking will be forgotten, but the London manufacturers will flourish. We need only look around with our eyes open to know that this is no fairy tale. The capitalistic structure of centralized production rests on the tombstones of its customers. Therefore, judged from the point of view of its effect on human beings, centralized production may be appropriately described as an enslaving, parasitic, or as Tagore would have it cannibalistic system. Once the victim realises the true situation, bestirs himself and sets about supplying all his own needs, the capitalist's reign is doomed.

AN EMANCIPATING SYSTEM

As against this, a method of production and consumption which will awaken the people to realise their own possibilities will be an emancipatory, creative or evolutive system. Our villages can meet their wants in two ways, (1) provide what they need by their own efforts, and (2) forego such of what they need as cannot be supplied by themselves. The reaction will be progressive self-reliance and self-advancement, though in the beginning the so-called standard of living may appear low. Our goal is a state where the villagers will supply all their own requirements and those of the city people. Their effort to do so will bring employment to millions and make for a better circulation of money. This is the only permanent way of dispelling poverty and creating wealth.

FREEDOM

What shall we do with political freedom even if it is given as a gift ? It will be meaningless as we shall not be able to turn it to good account. As our people learn to produce all that is needed by the country they will acquire self-reliance which is the basis of freedom, while dependence on others is the essence of slavery. When the villagers have become self-reliant and attain freedom, they will be able to look after themselves. Their *panchayats* will function, they will settle their own disputes and sanitation, build their own roads, run their schools and, to an extent, tax themselves and thus govern themselves. If we are not prepared to take up all this responsibility our second state will be worse than the first.

As a corollary to this, such discipline and initiative as may be generated by self-directing and regulating villages will enable us to put up a non-violent barrage of defence against any foreign aggression, without submitting to the humiliating experience of begging other nations to help defend our own hearths and homes.

THE SEED OF IMPERIALISM

We usually understand by imperialism a state where one nation holds down another in bondage so as to obtain some benefit to itself at the cost of the subjection of the other. We may have the spirit of such imperialism without having to cross national, political or geographical boundaries. The essence of imperialism is often found in even a single individual. When reduced to its lowest terms, it arises out of the desire to gain something for one-self at the cost of another. Wherever we find this we have the element of imperialism.

In centralized industries under private ownership we find this spirit in a virulent form. Therefore, every country that takes to this form of economic organization will in the end produce imperialism, and not freedom. It is a double edged sword. It injures both him who uses it and the victim. It flourishes only with outside compulsion and external discipline.

Naturally, to such an evil the antidote is one's own initiative and self-discipline. The promotion of decentralized industries helps us to develop both. No country can then enslave us without our active co-operation. If we can generate sufficient internal discipline to resist any external enticement, we shall be able to attain and retain freedom but until then we are doomed to be slaves.

Imperialism governs from outside, and is based on violence and fear. But true freedom is an outcome of self-discipline, non-violence and love. Where the latter condition exists there can be no high or low, rich or poor, but all men will be brethren.

We are witnessing with our own eyes the ultimate outcome of the spirit of imperialism. Germany, Japan, Great Britain and U.S.A. are all fighting so that each may control the world's resources for its own benefit. We shall find this true, if we probe deep enough behind the ostensible causes set forth by each combatant. Imperialism amongst nations or within nations or between individuals leads to destruction, enmity and violence. Do we want this state of affairs to condition our lives ?

As long as the selfish desire to benefit from another's toil is present amongst us neither Premier Churchill nor Sir Stafford Cripps can help us.

We are held in bondage so that we may supply the raw materials to the mills of Great Britain and afford a well-controlled market for their products. Therefore, the moment we begin to utilize our raw materials ourselves and supply all our needs, the foundation of imperialism is blasted.

Though the prescription appears simple enough the medicine is hard to take as it demands a considerable degree of self-control and presupposes self-discipline. As things are, village-made articles appear expensive as there is a greater degree of distribution of wealth included in the price while the apparent cheapness of imported mill-made articles is due to a small share in the booty of the manufacturer and his Government. Are we to be led away by this small share in the loot ? Village-made articles are sometimes crude, largely due to our neglect of the villagers. Shall we abandon these for the small satisfaction we may get from the use of standardized products ? These are the small crosses we have to bear in the initial stages to attain Swaraj ultimately. Do these loom too large on our horizon, dull our distant vision, and distort our judgement to such an extent that we prefer the foreign yoke with fineries to Swaraj ? Better is a dry morsel and freedom therewith, than a house full of so-called good things with bondage.

To the extent to which rural India supplies the major and primary needs of the people, to that extent we shall attain Swaraj. Both producers and consumers can help in this programme. Every man, woman and child can take part in this fight against imperialism.

CHAPTER 7 THE FUNCTION OF WORK

Should our purpose be one of making work for many ? If it should, then what is the virtue in making work ? Is it charity ? Is work a curse or a blessing ? What does work bring to man ? Do men improve by working or they wear out ? We shall spend a few moments considering these and similar questions.

The supplying of good wholesome food material and other honest products is in itself a worthy object. It is social work of a high order especially in these days of adulteration. Finding employment for the unemployed may also be considered a praise-worthy humanitarian work. If we stop at these, have we fulfilled our mission in life ? If work were only a matter of supplying goods, why not go in for mass production whereby larger quantities may be supplied ? Work for work's sake idealises drudgery. Drudgery is to be minimised, and one who makes drudges of men is no benefactor. Then what is it we are after ?

Work as Religion :

One of the things that distinguishes man from beast is religion. By religion people generally understand ceremonial worship. If a man is truly religious, his every action should declare the glory of his Maker. Ordinarily understood, religion occupies only a little fraction of man's waking hours. Most of his time is spent in work. Practically all his thought is concentrated on it and his life consists of what he does.

This being so, work is even more consequential than ceremonial religion. We may almost say that work is the practical side of religion. To deny man his opportunity to work is therefore to deny him the privilege of being a full-fledged human being if religion differentiates man from beast. Looked at this way, work denied to man is like denying him entry into a temple. Economically, the unemployed are like the untouchables in society. Both stages are equally degrading to man. Banishing unemployment is like throwing open the doors of a temple to everybody.

A little clear thinking will show that from a practical point of view the function that work plays in society is even more important than that of ceremonial religion. It is easy to profess to love God in the abstract, but it is difficult to show one's love of God in one's everyday dealings with one's neighbour. The first represents the ordinary conception of religion and the latter the real function of work. If we do not love the brother we have seen, how shall we love God whom we have not seen ?

From this aspect, work is, as already said, even more important than ceremonial religion. But work has not always been looked upon as sacred.

Analysis of Work :

When we analyse work we do not find it a curse in itself. It has two important components—(1) the germ of growth, *i.e.* an element which makes for the development and happiness of the individual and (2) drudgery. Just as any seed may have the pericarp and the starch and even as any balanced diet needs both the concentrates and the roughage to make it wholesome, work needs both its component parts to enable one to benefit by it. As the saying goes, genius is one per cent inspiration and ninety nine percent perspiration. Without the perspiration or drudgery the inspiration cannot become effective. One has to have both to benefit by it. The drudgery part of work is essential to enable one to grow through work. A musician has to practise hundreds of hours on his instrument before he can perform on the stage.

Before a person becomes a scientist he has to labour for years in a laboratory and cultivate a sense of smell which will appreciate sulphurated hydrogen. These are inevtiable. Therefore, there can be growth only when the pleasurable part of work is combined with the drudgery. One who avoids drudgery will not gain by the pleasurable part only. Though one may enjoy it for a time one will begin to deteriorate after a while. When properly used, work itself functions as an outlet to the personality of the individual, it gives expression to that which is highest in man and develops his faculties. Whatever ideals, principles or religion a man may adhere to are reflected in his everday work. The reaction on the individual is perhaps much more important than the work done because it goes to develop human personality and thereby contributes to human progress.

Naturally, the drudgery part of work being unpleasant, human nature being what it is, there is always an attempt to avoid it or shift it on to someone else. But as no one is willing to take on drudgery for what it is, it becomes necessary to use coercion. If we set out merely to enjoy life we shall have to force someone else to take up the drugery part of work at the threat of the taskmaster's whip. Western nations made no attempt to evercome this divorce of the pleasurable germ from the drudgery part of work.

On the other hand, they definitely set out to glorify the pleasures of life which in itself means enslavement of others.

It was on such a philosophy of work that the ancient empires of Greece and Rome worked, shifting the unpleasant part of activity, by which pleasure can be had, on to the captives made into slaves. Similarly, during the feudal days the lords got drunk and serfs laboured. It was a sign of distinction to enjoy without working. Again, under the financial regime, the capitalist and the executives enjoyed at the cost of the factory drudge. When we come to the political age, we see empires enjoying at the cost of their colonies. The whole of this system is based on violence. Without violence no nation can shift its drudgery to other nations and convert them into "hewers of wood and drawers of water".

Forms :

According to Aristotle, slavery was ordained by Nature. Work devoid of its opportunity for self expression becomes drudgery, and slavery is the result. In consequence, the civilizations of Greece and Rome regarded work as an evil. In the measure in which a man could free himself from work or heavy toil, he gained social status. Slaves were ordained by nature to toil away. Under such ideals these civilizations collapsed. We shall find the same view point on work projected into the economic organization of the West.

We may divide our daily activities into three kinds :

1. Exertion under external order.
2. Exertion for its own sake.
3. Exertion with a self-chosen purpose.

The first form is slavery and saps the vital energy of human life. The second form is one in which there is physical development or pleasure as in games and play, but it is in the third we find true work with an aim which leads to the development of higher faculties in man.

If work for work's sake were good, then indeed slavery would be goodness itself in "pill form". What is then wrong with slavery ? Initiative is taken away and this leads to decay of personality. Thus the seed of mental development is sterilized. All that is left is drudgery. In its proper place drudgery is no evil, but by itself it is a drag. Just as for good digestion we need a good deal of roughage, we need 90 or 95% of drudgery to get the best out of work, and just as if we eat only the roughage and no food our stomachs will suffer and life may become extinct, so also if we have only drudgery, and no initiative, all progress will be at an end and society will die. The toil of slavery is not work but drudgery, and hence it spells death. If we give drudgery to the masses, as is done under the methods of large scale productin, there is nothing but social death awaiting us. The irksomeness in slavery is largely due to external compulsion having taken the place of willing co-operation or personal initiative. We have seen that the first type leads to deterioration and therefore, taking into consideration the wear and tear of human life, slavery is the most extravagant form of labour.

Status :

In a predatory stage, work is looked down upon. A person is regarded clever if he can acquire the greatest amount of material gain with the least amount of exertion. Physical work is certainly at a discount. It is because of this view point that exploitation has gained ground. The mentally alert, in order to save themselves from work, have lorded it over the less assertive ones whom they have forced to work for them. Further, in this stage, work is looked upon as a means of acquiring wealth. Wealth in its turn is not sought after for means of providing the primary needs of life but for the acquisition of control over the lives of other men or, in other words, for power. Wealth in this sense is a dangerous instrument in the hands of the ambitious, for it leads to the enslavement of weaker persons. Just as a steel blade may be used as a dagger to stab an enemy or as a knife to cut an edible fruit, work may be either a deadly weapon or a faithful servant of man. Under Western methods of production, work leads to concentration of power, and that is an unfailing proof that work in the West is misdirected into wrong channels. It does not matter whether the concentrated power is used for good or evil. If the means are bad the end cannot justify them. Both under Capitalism and under Communism, work aims at or results in concentration of power. In Capitalism power is concentrated in the hands of the Capitalist and in Communism in the hands of the few who run the State. Workers under such circumstances exist to work; man is regarded as made for work and he ends up by becoming a slave. He labours, and someone else gets the power his labour generates. Such work saps the life of man, and leaves him exhausted at the end of the day. This is the part played by work in all socalled industrially advanced countries of the world today. The working man functions as "dumb driven cattle." All initiative is taken out of him; he becomes a cogwheel in the economic machinery. With the deprivation of initiative, he loses interest and all sense of responsibility. He ceases to think, and the more he gets into the meshes of the powerful, the less resisting power he possesses to escape from the disaster awaiting him.

We need not dwell long on the second type. It is essential within limits. Play has its place in a well-ordered life, but if it assumes the place of a main objective in life then, "all play and no work will make Jack a dull boy". The lower strata of ancient Greece and Rome were slaves and passed out of existence as animals do. The higher strata of society took to play and amusement and they developed physically but met with ultimate destruction morally and spiritually. Human body needs drudgery. Therefore where work is confined only to the pleasant part even the needed drudgery is given in a pleasant form as games. This is the reason why we find the West has laid much emphasis on games such as tennis, cricket, football, etc.

Cultural :

It is only in the last type that we find man at his best. What builds our character is not the great decisions of life but, the solutions we come to on small questions from day to day. Work absorbs most of our waking hours, and many of the problems connected with work and our dealings with our fellow men are what determine the nature of our life. Therefore, it behoves us to sit up and take note of what our work makes of us. If we analyse world history correctly we shall find that civilizations were what they were because of the nature of the economic life of the people. Religion may have infused ideals, but work was the laboratory in which they were tried out. Therefore, work can play a much wider part in the development and growth of a nation than institutional or ceremonial religion, and yet how much conscious thought do leaders bestow on this formidable force ? Properly directed, work affords facilities for the development of patience, perseverance, initiative, creativeness and originality and with it self-confidence, a sense of responsibility, accuracy and an eye for detail and fine finish. Work is indeed a school for life. What food is to the body that work is to the faculties of man.

In both Capitalism and Communism, or as a matter of that, in all large-scale productions, the worker becomes a mere hand where head and heart are hardly exercised. In such economic organizations, culture has to be acquired outside work, so far as this is possible. Psychologically, this is an altogether artificial way of introducing culture into people who have been deprived of it through the natural channel of work. If this is to be rectified and work be made a means of obtaining culture, or in other words, a means of developing one's personality in all its three aspects of intelligence, character and artistic sense, then it is obvious that work cannot be planned and dictated from the centre, but must be decentralized. In this undertaking of setting work back in it rightful place, the greatest difficulty is to overcome the ideas that have been instilled into the people by a false system of education including wrong standards of value. The Village Industries Association, which seeks to restore work to its proper place in the life of the nation, has, therefore to work against great odds. It has not only to change the present day ideology in regard to work—a matter which cannot be done in a day—but it has also to provide new methods of work. Inventions reflect the mental attitude with which problems are approached. As already said, in the last two centuries, machinery has been so devised as to concentrate power. We have to discountenance the use of such aids to production but in time we hope to substitute these by such tools as will lessen drudgery without concentrating power.

When England took to centralized methods of production, Great Britain was not an Empire. Its economic life was based on decentralized methods of production. She was a highly cultured country with a strong moral background. Even now when we think of her great contribution to the progress of man we have to look back to the period before the Industrial Revolution. The best of her literature Shakespeare, Milton and such like were Elizabethian; in Art, men of the type of Sir Joshua Reynolds flourished prior to the nineteenth century. Sir Christopher Wren and his peers in architecture never saw a textile mill to afford them inspiration. Moral giants like Latimer who were British Satyagrahis, who were prepared to lay down their lives for their convictions, never saw the power of the steam engine. We may say the Victorian Era was the darkest age in British History culturally whatever its glamour may have been financially and materially. After the Industrial Revolution Great Britain gained the whole world but lost its soul.

A greater achievement will be to combat the prevailing idea of work and instil into people's minds that work must have as its end the well-being of the worker.

In work of the type ordained by nature, there is little use for so called leisure. People will find it much easier to spend their time working under congenial conditions than to use leisure profitably. To use leisure properly, one has to have a high degree of self-discipline which is one of the valuable products of true work. If in the course of our daily work we get ample room for the expression of our personality, then there will be no need for leisure. Of course, there will be physical weariness which is healthy and which needs repose and relaxation in sleep and rest.

The moment we shift the emphasis from men to the material, we lose sight of the true function of work. If in a training institution young men spend their efforts in handling planes, hammer and chisel, they may waste wood but they are developing their muscles and skill. On the other hand, if they are made to feed sawing machines and to use their time in producing fine furniture by elaborate machinery the emphasis is on material gain and not on the training. Is finely carved and finished furniture more important than the skill of the young men ?

If we would save man from being degraded into a beast or an automaton, we have to face this situation and find a solution, wherein work will cease to be a means of concentrating wealth and power but will become a means of distributing wealth. If this is achieved, there will not be the meteoric careers of millionaires but we shall have a few more annas put into the pockets of the starving millions. This will increase the real wealth of the nation even if the money value be the same. If one lakh of rupees be concentrated in the hands of one person, the utility of that amount to the person who possesses it is nothing as compared to the utility of the same one lakh, if it were distributed among one hundred thousand poor people and found them their daily bread. Today all work is directed towards producing the articles by which the largest profits can be made rather than to meeting man's primary requirements. Therefore, the poor man's needs are forgotten while there is a glut in the rich man's luxuries.

The idea that production should aim at supplying the needs of the worker, rather than at acquiring wealth or power, is what underlies the programme of the Village Industries that meet the primary needs of the people such as the production of articles of food, clothing and shelter. This is again seen in the All India Spinners' Association programme of self-sufficiency under which the spinners have to provide themselves with clothing out of their own spinning.

From our point of view, any wrong use of work is sin and causes sorrow. Western organizations have, as repeatedly pointed out, looked upon work as a means of accumulating wealth *i. e.*, gathering in the available purchasing power from everybody to obtain control over the lives of men. This has naturally led to jealousies and violence. Can anything else be expected ? Unless we bestir ourselves and restore work to its proper place and man to his natural dignity and allow work to develop the masses, there is little hope of finding persons who will be able to bear responsibility and steer the helm of state to peace and prosperity.

Fatigue :

If only we can detach ourselves from turmoil of the modern world, we shall see clearly the havoc caused by the unnatural "pack-type" of organization. If the urge is from within, his work should leave the worker a better man. Nature has so planned it that we improve by working if our work follows the natural order. For example, if a person who has the talents of an artist is made to drive a car, it will be disastrous to the occupants of that car. He will only attain his full height if he is allowed to follow his natural inclination. We can tell by the effect work produces on a person if he is in his proper place. But when we look at the workers under "pack-type" what do we find ? Are they better human beings for their toil ? On the contrary, we find a set of men and women whose life and energy have been sapped. The diagnosis is simple. There is a parasite feeding on their lives. They suffer from nervous disorders as we have already noted in the second chapter. Therefore their method of production is unnatural and must lead ultimately to decay and destruction.

Sir Cyril Burt, University of London Psychologist says, "Human intelligence in Britain is declining at an alarming rate. If the present rate of decline in England continues for another fifty years the number of young people of superior ability would be halved and the number of feeble minded would be doubled". He has undertaken intelligence tests over a period of forty years.

What, we have to ask ourselves, is all this pressure of life for ? The "pack-type" believes in increasing the standard of of living. What does this mean but a hankering after an extension of its market ? If by a higher standard of life is meant increasing the multiplicity of wants, has this, as is so often claimed, brought about happiness or freedom from drudgery ? Has the working woman in England with her "higher standard of life" exemplified by a carpeted floor and a larger house with furniture, any greater freedom from drudgery than our Indian sister with a cowdunged floor and a *charpai* ? If anything the Enghish working woman has perhaps a greater amount of everyday drudgery, for the carpets have to be brushed, the dishes and plates washed and wiped, while the furniture and glass windows need dusting and polishing, and her linen has to be washed and ironed. Has she not really increased her drudgery ? Is her happiness any greater ? One thing, however, her higher standard of life has assuredly done. It has created a demand for the capitalist's production. More building and furnishing materials are sold; there is a demand for vacuum cleaners to clean carpets and so on. Is not then even consumption under the "pack-type" an enslavement to drudgery ? The greater our material possessions, the greater our bondage to earth. The advocate of a "higher standard of life" will do well to realise that he is an agent for the sale of the capitalist's goods. We lead such artificial lives under the "pack-type" that we lose sight of the natural order of things and thereby fall an easy prey to the wiles of exploiters.

CHAPTER 8 MORAL ISSUES OF RICHES

There are many forms of wealth—wealth of character, wealth of knowledge, wealth of possessions etc. Each of these has several characteristics. We shall restrict ourselves here to considering the different aspects of material wealth.

Under the urge of capitalistic economy, we have been taught to look at wealth purely from the material aspect. If you have money and you exchange it for some goods you stand in need of, there is an end of it. No further questions need be asked as long as what you get satisfies your material wants, and you are told, you have got your money's worth. If men were mere animals, and there were no such thing as a soul, matters may end here. There can be no talk of consciences, "tainted money" or "trusteeship".

Fortunately most of us are not so materialistic. We understand, may be vaguely, what rights and duties are. We do have a conscience, dull though it may be, and we dimly realise the moral and spiritual make up of human beings. This being so, our economic life is capable of being projected into the eternal on the spiritual level. Generally, economics have been considered too mundane to have any moral values. Scholars, especially in England, have attempted to deal with it in an abstract, scientific way, as they would study the Laws of Gravitation, with the result that in Marshall and Pigou, economic theory has gone to seed in mathematical formulae rather than being presented as a fascinating psychological study of human nature. If we stop to think, we should realise that at least unsophisticated persons do act as though there was more to economics than material values as the following examples will show :

There are various standards of value used by the general run of people.

(1) Certain articles are valued, not for any material reason but purely out of sentiment. An old chair or a table, associated with the memory of a loving parent, may be too precious to be computed in terms of money.

(2) In a brassware shop when a *lota* is weighed and priced according to the amount of metal in it, we have an instance of intrinsic material value.

(3) If anyone offered for sale a gold necklace that had been stolen from a child, whose neck had been wrung to get it, there will be very few persons brazenly materialistic enough to buy it, were the facts known. The price will not be the determining factor in the transaction. This is the moral aspect.

(4) When a person, like Gandhiji, who can afford to use silk and gold-laced *dhotis* uses a *langoti* of coarse cloth, as by so doing he shares the lot of the majority of his fellow beings, he rises to the spiritual plane.

Each economic transaction reflects the self, emotional, pragmatic, base, uplifting or idealistic, according to the standards of value we apply.

On the acquisition side, if a person has made his pile by occupations which are deemed anti-social, such as running toddy shops or brothels, the money is said to be tainted. We generally stop short of these. We rarely apply any moral standards where doubtful practices had been resorted to as in the case of a lawyer or a medical man who uses his case as a source of income, without being solely guided by what is best for his client or patient. And still less are the ways of "successful" business men scrutinised.

The spending side is almost completely bereft of all higher standards of value. A buyer hardly realises he owes any duties at all in his everyday transactions. Just as much of the guilt of murder is attached to the necklace wrung from a child, every article in the bazar has moral and spiritual values attached to it. To put in a sort of legalistic language, the seller transfers his title, good or bad, to the buyer. Hence it behoves us to enquire into the antecedents of every article we buy. This is a grave responsibility. How many of us are discharging our duties faithfully when we do our marketing daily ? If we buy an article which had been produced by paying wages which are below subsistence level, we are buying an article with human life attached to it. Horrible though this may seem a little dispassionate reasoning will reveal the ghastly truth. When an article is produced by a machine that machine wears out as it works and in time it becomes unusable. Hence, the wear and tear of the machine plus repairs and upkeep, has to be charged and spread over the number of articles produced by the machine. Man is a machine. If a potter makes pots, the price of the pots should be all costs including the maintenance charges of the potter and his folks. Maintenance is not merely what keeps him alive but should include sufficient to keep him in a fit working condition; if not, the cheap pots will include part of his wasting self. Higher price, when necessitated by the payment of adequate wages, is a thing to be aimed at and no buyer should grudge paying it. Hence, those of us, who apply human standards of value, have to enquire into all aspects of manufacture. It is an arduous task and it becomes almost impossible for ordinary persons to undertake it when the articles come from far off countries. Therefore, it is that we have to restrict our purchases to articles made within our cognizance. This is the moral basis of "Swadeshi".

When there are competing articles in the market, and we buy a foreign, cheap product, in preference to a home-made article, we are party to creating unemployment and poverty in our land. If we cannot afford to satisfy our needs by paying proper prices for home-made articles, it would be a spiritual act to restrain ourselves from using foreign substitutes. However good a thing may be materially, if it does not appeal to our moral and spiritual standards, we should reject it. If our moral consciousness is strong, it will need not effort to forego the satisfaction of a want. If you go to buy sugar and find beautiful cubes of white sugar made in mills, and side by side with it somewhat unattractive cottage-made loose sugar, to your fastidious eye the cottage-sugar may look dirty but if your moral eye is open, the apparently clean mill-sugar will be undoubtedly filthy. "For there is nothing from without a man that entering into him can defile him, but the things which come out of his heart, those are they that defile the man". Most of us are wide awake materially. Shall we not strive to develop our moral and spiritual consciousness ? Even if the sugar be dirty it can be purified with a little trouble but can we afford to lose our soul ?

We do not live unto ourselves and the more we realise the repercussions of our actions on our neighbours and strive to act according to the highest we are capable of, the more shall we advance in our spiritual development.

CHAPTER 9 THE PLACE OF WOMEN

While man possesses initiative in a great measure and is venturesome, woman is by nature much more conservative and conventional. Generally speaking, man is objective while woman is subjective. If we may use such an analogy, man may be said to belong to the "pack" and woman to the "herd" type. This being so, each sex partakes of the characteristic of its type. We noted that Eastern men, whom we regard as falling under the "herd" type, do not follow leadership easily in committees and such like. Women find it even more difficult than men to work in committees. Because of the "herd" type mentality, they are conventional, and religion and social customs appeal to them more than to men. In the same way, Eastern men are said to be ritualistic, more religious and obey convention and regulation more readily than the men of the West, for the "herd" type is more law-abiding than the "pack" type. Even in the "pack" type, woman is less self-centred than man, for her love covers the family.

Hence, in all matters requiring the qualities of the "pack" type man is better suited to take the lead where initiative and adventure are necessary.

The present system of production does not take into consideration the role that is assigned to woman by nature. It will be generally admitted that by their very make up they are the custodians of a nation's culture and project into the future the achievements of the present generation. In primitive times consumption was controlled by women, while supplies were in the hands of men. If women did the cooking, men provided food materials. If women needed a home, men provided the wherewithal in the form of bamboos, thatch, mud walls, etc. In the language of economics the woman was the creator of demand and the man's place was that of the supplier. As evolution advanced under the "herd" type, woman was given a place in the social control of production, and thus the rules of conduct and regulatory machinery were provided for. We find even today in India, inspite of the deplorable state of culture and the depth of ignorance and superstition to which women have sunk in our country, that they still play an overwhelming part in the everyday life of the nation. However advanced in his views and however cultured a man may be, it is often his wife's superstition and ignorance that rules the home and he pleads his inability to go against the dictates of the mother or wife. This is one of the main reasons why even though a large number of Indian men have acquired modern ways of living, yet their homes are often to be found in insanitary and unhygienic conditions. Unless women are culturally equal to men, there will be a disparity and social life will follow the level of development of women. It will be next to impossible for men to put their ideals into practice unless their womenfolk also see eye to eye with them. Nature has endowed woman with certain faculties which are largely dormant in man, such as intuition. Hence their contribution to the economic sphere is bound to be different and the role they play will be distinct and will not overlap.

In the "pack-type" woman's place in the economic sphere was largely ignored. Under the dynasty of might she was merely a cave man's captive and her sexual allurements have made and unmade empires. Under the dynasty of finance she became the emblem of the social status of the financier. In her dress and manners she displayed the ostentatious mode of life made possible by necessary appurtenances drawn from all parts of the world. Her main function seemed to be to fight for such social rights as befitted the income of her man. With the advent of the machine, she fell further and became either a mannequin, advertising the wares of machine production which she began to consume as a result of high pressure salesmanship, or she became "emancipated" to the extent that she entered factories as a producing hand, where the machine-owner exploited her lack of staying power by giving her lower wages. When labour came into power, she was assigned an equal place with man as a producer. But in all these various forms of "pack-type" economic organizations she has not found the true place assigned to her by nature as the creator of demand and the custodian of national culture. Machine-owners produce articles and suggest to women that they should consume them and women have been following fashions blindly and by readily walking into this trap have become mere consumers. Today, whatever may be the claim for equalityof the sexes and whatever may be the result of enfranchisement of women in the political sphere, they remain an excellent market for the consumption of machine-made goods. They have abdicated their natural role to the profit motive which has now ascended the throne. It alone directs economic production and has assumed the part that should have been played by women had they realised their true calling. Man is working single-handed in the economic sphere as a supplier without the aid of his partner who should have by her demand laid down the lines on which production should proceed. The enormous maladjustment we find in the world today is in no small measure due to women not occupying their proper place in the economic sphere. Even in the "pack-type", unless woman assumes her rightful place and dethrones the profit motive, there will be no hope for a natural order of economic production. Once, however, women take their proper place, the subsidiary activities dependent on the home will fall into proper alignment and this will surely lead to human progress.

Woman has proved herself an easy prey to psychological suggestions made by advertisers. If women will assert themselves and become discriminating buyers, even if they do nothing else, we shall find a transformation in the variety of goods produced. After all the bulk of the commodities produced and put on the market are for the home and therefore come within the purview of the woman who is the homemaker.

CONSUMER'S DUTIES

Often buyers are only concerned with satisfying their own requirements as near as possible and as cheaply as they can. This way of going about the business is to shirk one's duties. What are the duties of an efficient consumer or buyer ? When buying an article of everyday use one has to take account of the full repercussions of one's transaction.

(1) One should know where the article comes from.
(2) Who makes the article ?
(3) From what material ?
(4) Under what conditions do the workers live and work ?
(5) What proportion of the final price to they get as wages ?
(6) How is the rest of the money distributed ?
(7) How is the article produced ?
(8) How does the industry fit into the national economy ?
(9) What relation has it to the other nations ?

DISCRIMINATE BUYING

If the buyer has to make her influence felt, the further afield she goes for her goods, the less will be the power of her influence at such distance, the less the chances of her information on the various points raised being accurate, and the less will be her personal interest. If the goods come from a source which may be tainted with exploitation, either of sweat labour or of the political, financial or economic hold over other nations, or classes, or races, then the buyer of such goods will be a party to such exploitation, just as a person who buys stolen articles from a *chore bazar* creates a market for stolen goods and thus will be encouraging the art of stealing. Therefore, any one who buys goods indiscriminately is not discharging her full responsibility when the sole criterion of her buying is merely the low price or the good quality of the goods. Hence, we should buy goods only from sources from which full information is readily available and which source can be brought under our influence; otherwise we shall have to shoulder a share of the blame for sweated labour, political slavery, or economic stranglehold. We cannot absolve ourselves of all blame by merely pleading ignorance in regard to the source.

If the raw materials for making cocoa are obtained from plantations on the West coast of Africa which use some form of forced native labour, are carried by vessels on sea routes monopolised or controlled by violence, manufactured in England with sweated labour and brought to India under favourable customs duties enforced by political power, then a buyer of a tin of cocoa patronises the forced labour conditions in the West coast of Africa, utilizes the navy and so partakes in violence, gains by the low wages or bad conditions of workers in England and takes advantage of the political subjection of India. All this responsibility and more also is put into a little tin of cocoa !

Are we prepared to shoulder this grave responsibility and pander to our palate or shall we content ourselves with a cup of nutritious milk drawn from a well-kept cow at our door ? These considerations are not far-fetched but actual. Anyone who looks on life seriously and as a trustee cannot afford to ignore these far-reaching consequences of her actions.

If we are not able to do this by ourselves we should draft in the help of bodies like the A. I. S. A. or the A. I. V. I. A. which certify certain products for sale. It is for this reason that Khadi should be bought at the certified Bhandars.

SWADESHI

If we feel it is beyond us to guarantee the concomittant results of all our transactions, it necessarily follows that we must limit our transactions to a circle well within our control. This is the bed rock of Swadeshi. Swadeshi is no rabid political slogan. It is circumscribed by our own limitations. The smaller the circumference, the more accurately can we gauge the results of our actions and more conscientiously shall we be able to fulfil our obligations as trustees.

MERIT OF TRUE BUYING

These considerations will naturally restrict our field of selection of goods and therefore will entail the curbing of the satisfaction of our wants. When you go to buy a *saree* the shopman may place before you endless attractive varieties of silks from Belgium, Paris and other places at very reasonable prices, but as a trustee you are prompted to buy the coarse Khadi cloth spun and woven by your poor neighbour. It is comparatively expensive, heavy to wear and not artistic enough for your taste. You will be fulfilling your duty by deciding on the Khadi in preference to the finery from abroad. This means a great sacrifice.

This control of self is our *tapasya*. Tapasya does not consist in sitting on a board of nails or putting a pin through the cheeks. In everyday life, when we forego a want or put up with the inconveniences of a restricted satisfaction in the pursuance of a principle of life we are performing *tapasya* no less ardently than the great rishis who have renounced the world and chosen the life of the recluse. We find this ideal set out in all religions. "Take up thy cross and follow me". Whenever we stand for a principle there will be a cross to take up. It is not a beautifully carved ivory one or a golden one embeded with gems which can be hung round one's neck on a gold chain, but is a real heavy cross which has broken the back of many a well meaning stalwart. But there is merit to be earned from the effort.

This sacrifice, tapasya or cross will take many forms in our endeavour to follow the spirit of Swadeshi. When you go to buy salt you are tempted by the purity and the convenient containers in which Cerebos salt is offered and the attractive manner in which it runs out of the container will almost make you decide in favour of it as you glance at the alternative of buying the black looking, dust laden, pebble-like country salt kept in open heaps in dirty gunny bags. It requires a strong character to resist taking the easier course, buy the country salt, dissolve it and purify it at home. With a little tapasya you can convert it into a purer article than the Cerebos variety. An American woman doctor always buys gur from the bazar, boils and cleans it, and keeps it in liquid form for children's use, not because she loves the village industry but because she prefers it to sugar on nutritive grounds. There are many reasons why we, more than this American sister, should take particular care to patronise such industries. Have we that steadfastness of purpose ?

Similarly, when sales facilities such as credits, sending on approval, providing of samples, execution of orders promptly to which capitalistic methods of production and high pressure salesmanship have made us accustomed, are lacking we shall again feel disgusted if we do not whip up our altruistic self into following our goal regardless of difficulties. We may rest assured that it will not be always thus. Our artisans who had produced goods which could not and cannot be copied by machinery, have fallen low as victims of unfair methods of competition, as their flanks were not guarded by dauntless customers. Shall we not now gather round those whom we had let down in the past and enable them to get on their feet again ? Once they recover their balance we can regain the conveniences we now associate with foreign and capitalistically produced and marketed goods.

REASON FOR DECAY OF INDUSTRIES

The above paragraph contains a grave confession that we, the buyers, have betrayed the artisans into the hands of their enemies by not guarding their flanks. I may be permitted to give an instance as to how the mentality that prefers to buy foreign goods progressively starves and kills our industries and ultimately reduces our country to poverty and degradation. Once, when I was touring in Travancore, I was looking into the conditions of the screw-pine mat-making industry. This industry was once very flourishing and now it is almost on its death-bed. There is apparently no reason for it as the workmanship is still excellent and the raw material is plentiful.

Screw-pine mats are made from the long leaves of a small hedge plant which is grown round the boundaries of each cottage. Cottages in Travancore generally stand in their own garden, detached from other dwellings, unlike the row of huts we find in other parts of the country. Men, women and children work with the leaf of this plant and produce beautiful, supple and soft mats which do not crack on drying, and can be washed clean. These were much in demand for sleeping on. The seniormost mat-maker was showing me and two friends round and was asking me to tell him why this industry was on its last legs and how it can be revived. I was hard put to, to answer his question. At last, he took us to his house and invited us to share his frugal fare. As we were washing he prepared a place for us on the vrandah of his house, and indicated my friends to take their seats on two screw-pine *asans* and assigned me a seat between them. As I caught sight of the mat spread for me, I stood amazed and stared at my host. He was bewildered, and enquired what was wrong. I replied, "I have discovered the cause of the decay of your industry. It has dawned on me this moment". He begged of me to tell him. I told him, "The cause is in your brain. It is a false standard of value". He was puzzled and asked me to explain. Then, I pointed to the two *asans* provided for my friends and enquired where he got them from. He said he had himself made them from the screw-pine leaves of his garden. The pointing to the tiger-printed mat on which I was to have taken my seat, I asked, "Where did you get this ?" He replied, he had bought it in the bazar. He thought of honouring me by spreading for me this gaudy Japanese mat. I pointed out to him that in his mind he valued that Japanese mat more than his own; if so, I asked, could he blame others for prefering Japanese products to his ? If everybody did the same as he did, his industry would naturally die. So I suggested that he should take the first step necessary to revive his industry by placing a higher value on his own handicraft and not patronise foreign articles in preference. This illustrates how our country has become degraded and poverty-stricken.

DIRECTING INDUSTRIES

Every sister who buys a foreign article takes the bread out of the mouth of our artisans by causing unemployment in our own land. This is a fundamental fact we have to realise and grasp. In Tamil we have a saying that a crew regards its own little ones as the most precious. But we have become foster parents to foreign and mill-industries, forgetting our own people. For witness look round your household and count the number of foreign and mill-made things you have got. The prices you have paid for them will indicate the extent of unemployment in our land you have been responsible for. Every pice you spend makes or mars an industry by directing wealth into it or away from it. Woman, the home maker, is the director of industries in the real sense. Is the educated to discharge this high calling ? Other nations, like Russia, Japan, Germany and Italy are encouraging their women to bring forth children so as to swell the ranks in their armies, thus reducing the nobility of motherhood to the level of stock-breeder or a soulless ammunition factory, and nurture their industries on the blood of their children when they wage war of economic purposes while we give our all to destroy what little we possess.

A MODERN YATRA

It may well be that sometimes we have to search for the goods we need. If you want a silk cord which is Indian-made you may have to wander from shop to shop and yet you may not find what you want and may have to rest content with a cotton substitute. If we have the necessary zeal all such efforts which prove apparently futile will not damp our spirits. We shall look upon such wanderings as *yatras*. There are people who measure their length on the ground all the way from Kanya Kumari to Kashi (Cape Comorin to Benares) as a means of earning merit. Can we be thwarted by anything less ?

We have to develop a burning religious zeal for the welfare of our villages.

> *"Can a woman's care*
> *Cease towards the child she bare ?*
> *Yes, she may forgetful be,*
> *Yet will I remember thee".*

Shall we remember our duty towards our fellow beings and fulfil our stewardship at all times and occasions ?

THE WAY OF FREEDOM

If we can resolutely refuse to buy foreign and mill-made goods, being content with what we can get from our neighbours, what interest will foreign nations have in holding us in subjection ? No doubt such an attitude will call for great fortitude under unparalleled privations both due to our own actions and those of others. Only when we develop such indomitable courage and unconquerable will can we come upto the standard of non-violence set by Gandhiji which will be necessary to free ourselves from foreign domination and ward off foreign invasions.

We cannot attain this except by denying ourselves taking up the cross daily and following steadfastly the principle of pursuing our duty to our fellowmen rather than enforcing our rights on them. By so doing we shall save the lives of millions and find our own through our *tapasya* and sacrifice. There is no doubt as to the capacity of women of our land to put forth this effort once they realise the need for it.

Will our sisters rise to the occasion and give up the easy and broad way that has led us to destruction, and discipline themselves to enter at the strait gate and follow the narrow way that will lead the nation to life abundant ? When women come into their own and play their role well, we shall realise fully the truth in the old adage that the hand that rocks the cradle rules the world.

CHAPTER 10 INTERNATIONAL STRIFE

In primitive days violence attached to hunting and fishing and to disputes over the sharing of property. In the "pack-type" aggression constitutes an essential feature. In the dynasty of might it forms the very basis for its successful working, the motive urge being personal aggrandisement, expansion and extension of rights, achievement of personal ambition or wreaking vengeance on an adversary.

Centralization and Himsa :

In the dynasty of finance, might and finance entered into partnership and bred imperialism. An armed power was necessary to maintain, safeguard and expand distant fields for the investment of capital from which good interest could be drawn. In the machine age, because of the heavy investment entailed in the instruments of production, it became necessary to produce as much as possible in a limited time because, if the machinery were allowed to be idle, the overhead charges, which are a constant factor, would assume a larger proportion of the cost of the finished articles. To reduce this it had to be distributed over as large a quantity of goods as possible. Therefore, the incentive for large production without regard to the existing market is in the very nature of a system of production based on expensive tools or instruments.

In addition to this, when individualistic control and free trade doctrines are promulgated, the desire for competitive production tends towards production without relation to the market. In both these cases it becomes necessary to find markets for the supplies that have been created. There is also the need to control distant raw material sources to enable the producer to obtain a steady flow of raw material. Division of labour is carried to an extreme. Therefore, to produce under this system, one has to conquer time and space, because the whole economic unit from the production of raw materials to the consumption of the finished article, covers the whole world. Unless the control of all the contributing factors is obtained so as to ensure a steady supply of raw materials at a speed demanded by the technical requirements of the plant and machinery for production at an economic speed and to ensure the disposal of goods so produced on profitable terms within reasonable time, no nation can be industrialized. Such control can only be secured by resorting to violence.

For instance, if Lancashire has to produce cloth, the mill itself is situated in Lancashire, where no cotton is grown. The mill forms the centre round which the whole world is made to rotate and subserve its purpose. The agricultural college in India investigates the kind of soil in which the type of cotton required by the mill can be grown. The researches of the college are directed towards producing, by cross breeding and the like, the quality of cotton which will give the best result for the mill. The farmers who may be cultivating food crops have to be induced to shift to cotton growing. When the cotton is grown, transport with favourable rates of freight to the ports has to be provided. At the port, facilities for loading in the form of quays and wharves have to be built. The shipping has to be regulated and safeguarded with naval base at Singapore and fortresses at Aden and Gibralter. To man these the army, the navy and the air force have to be maintained. Such centralized methods of production cannot be carried on for one day without the backing of the army, the navy and the air force. This Lancashire mill is an integral part of a world-wide organization. It is, therefore, imperative to control the agricultural college, the farmers, taxation, the railways, shipping routes etc. This cannot be done without the political domination of India and the routes that lead to it. This is on the production side. The organization does not end there.

A nation that is industrialized depends for its very existence on its sources of raw material and on markets for its finished articles. The control of these forms a veritable struggle for existence. These factors lead to the need for obtaining and retaining markets which end can only be achieved by keeping down or controlling other people by force. Anyone who interferes with the raw material source or with the market is like a person trying to snatch a bone from a hungry dog. Such interference leads to violence. In the case of labour organizations of production, because the power, control, and planning are centralized, a considerable amount of sanctions are needed for proper carrying out of plans. The urge for production, being external and not from within, is unnatural and therefore needs coercion and violence. Regulation is by force and the system itself being run much on the lines of capitalistic and individualistic methods of production can be converted at a moment's notice into any of the other forms of the "pack-type". Hence it attracts the attention of highly armed nations and as a means of protection it involves large scale armaments.

It is because of these reasons that at the present time Western nations are finding it impossible to bring about a peaceful regulation of affairs. All wars and international disturbances today have their roots in the "pack-type" economic systems of production and as long as these exist, it follows, as the effect the cause, that there must be and will be war. No amount of agreement between nations, however well-meant, will lead to disarmament. We have seen the impotency of resolutions passed by the League of Nations. In effect, this league has become a league of wolf-packs and cannot be converted into anything else so long as international relations are based on the present economic structure. If we in India also follow these types of economic organization, it will be next to impossible for us to avoid the consequences of such systems. Unfortunately, Japan has deviated from the "herd-type" of economic organization and has gone whole-heartedly into "pack-type" with the result that she has become as aggressive and imperialistic as any of the Western nations. "He who draws the sword will perish by the sword". Do we subscribe to the ideals that underlie methods of economic production as we see them in the West, or shall we evolve a type which will be different in its very nature from the "pack-type" by following the lines that have been laid down by the civilization that has grown up into our own country and as produced the "herd-type" of economic order ? In doing so it will not be necessary for us to follow in detail the original rules and regulations as they were made for a certain specific stage in evolution, and will not suit our purposes in the modern world, but it will be possible for us to evolve an order which will curb individual greed, increase production in relation to demand and confine it as well as its marketing to the needs of the people.

What is the situation in the world today ? The world is surcharged with violence. Nations are gnashing their teeth and snarling at each other under the clock of armed neutrality and an ostensible "peace". There is hidden hatred and enmity in every hand stretched out in "brotherhood". All talk of championing weak nations is motivated by selfishness, greed and avarice. Professions of a desire to civilize backward nations and to bring light and learning to those who sit in darkness are the excrescence of imperialism. In short, we see wolves stalking the land as lambs.

We noticed that the movements of dumb creatures are conditioned by search for food, and hunger is the urge behind their labours. They reap where they sowed not; they consume without producing. Their ferocity is increased in the same ratio as the scarcity of food. Or, in economic language, if such may be used, the intensity of the demand causes violence for supply is limited and competition for that which is available is sharpened.

The position is not very different when we come to man in the nomadic stage. He, like the animal, is not able to increase supply to meet the demand, but moves about from scarcity to plenty, and anyone who stands in his way falls a prey to his wrath. His production, if any, is very limited and his consumption is predatory, nature being generally the victim. The directive force which fashions his movements could again be said to be hunger in a larger sense *i. e.*, his very elementary and savage needs. He also finds that his demands are not always met by nature and when this is so there is competition and violence.

From the nomad we pass on to the agriculturist who for the first time, tries to equate supply with demand by aiding nature *i. e.*, by his production. Thus he is able to control supply. He is able to meet even his greater needs in the shape of food, clothing and shelter. He produces what he needs and consumes to his satisfaction. In this stage, as the diversity between demand and supply is not great, competition is curbed. There is no unwholesome pressure to increase consumption artificially and hence, the generation of violence is lessened. Supply follows demand and the production is to order *i. e.*, definitely directed towards satisfying an existing need. We may call it a "bespoken economic order". A man needs a pair of shoes and these are made especially to fit his feet and their shape. Only in this manner can the demand be fully satisfied. The ability or the ingenuity of the producer expands with the exacting nature of the demand and leads to the development of his skill and personality, and thereby contributes to the culture of the age. As long as the producer rises equal to the occasion and satisfies the demand there is no room for violence. Every one eats of his vine and of his fig tree and drinks the waters of his cistern and there is peace in the land.

In the "pack-type" the nomad's dependence on nature is forgotten. The agriculturist's attempt to supplement nature is carried to the other extreme and man celebrates his "conquest" over nature. Nature's forces are harnessed to serve man. Various devices to aid man in his activities have been invented. But here again he has overreached himself and the machine that was intended to be a servant has become the master thus reducing the bulk of mankind to abject slavery. Supply has made larger strides than demand. In the earlier stages the struggle was to increase the supply. Now over-production loudly calls for an increase in demand. Machinery spells standardization and large scale production. Even then this does not meet the demand correctly. A man in Bombay wants a pair of shoes. He goes into a shop and he is presented with footwear made in Northampton by a shoemaker who has never set eyes on the customer. The shoe manufacturer makes standard sizes and without trouble he easily multiplies the number. He does not wait for orders. Like pat-a-cake, the baker's man, he makes them as fast as he can and ships them to various parts of the world for sale. The supply comes into existence without knowledge of the extent of the demand and then, perforce the producer has to try and create it. The barefooted natives have to be "civilized" in order to be made to wear European shoes. This leads to violence. Again, in an industry like the steel industry powerful vested interests influence the Government to find outlets for their products. The Government seeks out "backward" peoples and builds railways and bridges for them while the children of the "backward" peoples are starving both physically and mentally. All these standardised products can be turned out in large quantities without much extra cost, and markets have to be found for these supplies. Such a state of things naturally leads to violence. Still worse is the case of the manufacturer of armaments (like the late Sir Basil Zaharoff) who is obviously interested in nurturing belligerent conditions which make for a boom period in his business. Violence is the very essence of his success. In the past, the directive forces which stimulated economic activity were the natural hunger of the savage and the nomad and the discomforts of the sensitive body of the agriculturist. These were nature's urge or goad. But now we have artificially to increase demand by habits cultivated by imitation or custom, so that the excess in production may be absorbed. Food, clothing and shelter were nature's demand but tobacco, lipstick, rouge and face powder are examples of the demand cultivated by imitation and custom. In many cases even if the consumer is indifferent, the producer, by modern methods of advertisement and other means of propaganda, persuades the public to use that which is unnecessary and has no real utility and may be even harmful but makes business for himself by the sale of his goods.

Thus we notice that the forces that formerly directed economic activity have shifted from the purpose of making good the shortage of supply to meeting the shortage of demand or, in other words, over production.

Supply and Demand and Himsa :

A study of history teaches us that when a people's demand is too difficult of satisfaction, their culture and civilization die. This situation may arise either by their inability to produce as in the Case of the Red Indians of America, or in the degeneration of the race as is seen in the downfall of every great empire. In the latter case, supply is increased by booty, loot and the exploitation of captured races as slaves, actually or constructively. To consume such predatory wealth the standards of life are artificially increased. Consumption takes place without production. Before long, such a civilization collapses as it has no back-bone. Predatory consumption is not conducive to growth but undermines the stamina of the people. A nation can flourish only as long as its demand can be met by its productivity. When there is not much disparity between demand and supply, the nation advances culturally. India, China and Egypt have to look back to the days of their agricultural civilization for the heyday of their cultures. In the West, the Industrial age produced a transitory culture during the mid Victorian Era, but it was not long before the supply went far ahead of the demand and steeped the world in that barbarism and despair wherein we find ourselves today. Indeed we can boast of knowledge and the advance of Science but that is not true culture. The pressure of life today is not conducive there to. There is no true leisure. We have to equate our supply and demand but not artificially. Until we are able to do this, violence will stalk the land. At present we are in a state of unstable equilibrium and our "civilization", such as it is, may topple over any moment.

We must inevitably check the artificial creation of demand. This cuts at the root of all imperialism. People have to evolve their own culture after their own fashion without any attempt on the part of the outsider to "bring civilization to backward people". Avarice, as a motive for production, has to be curbed and the extent of each person's economic activity has to be limited to his capacity in such a way that the weaker members are not exploited. Under capitalism, profit motive is allowed free play without regard to any other consideration. Goods are produced for immediate gain and in a manner which gleans the profits into a few pockets only. This leads to a shortage of necessaries, over production of luxuries and maldistribution of wealth, while the masses are reduced to undernourished machine feeders. This state of affairs has generated class consciousness resulting in the conflict of Capital and Labour. On the other hand, Soviet Communism has given up the profit motive but has intensified class hatred. Its working has resulted in a greater concentration of power than under capitalism where we get a concentration of wealth which is a lesser evil. The workers have little initiative which is a prerequisite for the formation of any culture. We should not aim at producing standardized man or a Robot but at developing the individuality of persons, however many may be their inconsistencies and incongruities. Material advancement is worth nothing when it is obtained either at the cost of the individual's personality, or at the cost of bringing about class hatred.

The production of supplies without reference to existing demands has created a complexity of circumstances. To dispose of the excess production markets have to be found. Competition has assumed a keenness never before known. To increase the consumers *i.e.*, the demand, it was necessary to complicate the lives of simple folks or to "civilize" them. The eagerness to capture markets and "civilize" backward peoples has led not only to jealousies between industrialized nations but also to resistance on the part of the victims and these have in their turn, led to armaments and violence on a scale in keeping with large-scale production which is the root of the trouble. In this turmoil there can be no room for real culture as all energies are concentrated either on feeding violence or on combating it.

Thus violence is the centre of the present organization or the foundation stone of the economic structure today. But it does not stop there. The ones who enjoy the pleasures through such dissection of work are not the masses. These common people will not take to violence naturally unless their understanding is warped and their sensitiveness blunted by a deliberate false propaganda. To achieve this it becomes necessary to glorify violence. This is done by giving a social status to those who are employed in applying violence on a "scientific" and mass scale and giving such violence religious recognition. A general, an admiral or any officer in the forces is given a social standing to obtain the respect of the common people. Memorials to such men when dead are placed in a place of worship to associate them with the saints and they are made national heroes by erecting of public statues and tombs.

Violence Glorified :

We should regard army men as scientific murderers and generals and admirals as arch-murderers. If we went into

St. Paul's Cathedral or the Westminster Abbey we shall see the monuments there to these arch-murderers. They have made the house of prayer into a den of arch-murderers. When we see the tattered banners of many a battle decorating those sacred walls do we not hear the reverberation of the echo of the two thousand year old cry "away with this man, release unto us Barabbas."

It is such "cultures" we find in Europe in battle array growling at each other at the present moment. What does this appeal to might mean ? Is this to make the world safe for democracy ? Or is it a war to end war ? We can no more cast out devils through the Prince of devils. All they that take the sword shall perish with the sword. What is all this degradation of the soul of man for ? It is to get raw materials and to control markets.

WHAT COST VIOLENCE

Man differs from the brute in his creative propensities. Man's progress, therefore, is measured by his creativeness. Modern warfare, on the other hand, is a competition in destructive capacity. What with centralized methods of production and standardization we are reaching a rate of destruction which bids fair to wipe out all civilization. Instead of men being occupied in supplying one another's wants today, they are engaged in destroying not only the productivity of the enemy but also their own, under the scorched earth policy.

In normal times we used to regard a crore of rupees as a colossal sum. A battleship of the type of the "Prince of Wales" costs about fifteen crores, and it is sent to the bottom of the sea in a few minutes. During a whole year the Government spends hardly twelve crores on education throughout India, barely three-quarters of the cost of a single battleship. A submarine boat will cost about fifty lakhs. With barely half this amount as capital the A. I. S. A. has provided work for years on end to about three lakhs of workers in over thirteen thousand villages, distributing in wages over fifteen lakhs of rupees amongst them. A single sixteen inch gun on a battleship costs about six lakhs. Two to three such guns will more than pay for all the famine relief given by Government in a year all over India, the expenditure on which score is about fifteen lakhs per year. Two shells fired from such a gun will more than pay the expenses of running the central office of the A. I. V. I. A. for a whole year. When we hear that ten bombers have been shot down it is equivalent to the loss of the whole capital of A.I. S. A. What Great Britain spends during a single day on this war will more than pay the expenses incurred by all the Provincial Governments and the Central Government for fifteen years in India on the promotion of Industries. Can India's poverty-striken masses afford to adopt a system of economic production which calls for periodical adjustment of equilibrium at such cost ?

PART III

THE SOLUTION

CHAPTER II INDUSTRIALIZATION

Agriculture had, as its complement in the past, various kinds of subsidiary handicrafts. In many industries payments were made to artisans in kind from agricultural products. In fact, such industries as were in existence were but the workshops of the farmers for supplying their tools, implements and other necessaries.

With the advance of civilization, daily requirements increased in quality, quantity and variety. To supply these, artisans carried on their trade until recent years in the vicinity of towns in the form in which it had been carried on in the past. The producer required little or no capital apart from what was needed for his simple tools, and even these, he often made himself. The question of marketing had not assumed the dignity of a problem. As there was a very small percentage of profits, the accumulation of capital was slow. Because of the existence of various industries and the rigidity of the division of labour as practised under the caste system the pressure on the land was comparatively little.

Disruption of India :

With the industrialization of Western countries, all this changed. India was turned into a market for goods from the West and utilized as an opportunity for the development of their industries. For instance, while the pressing need of India was canals for irrigation and transport, railways were built to afford opportunities of development for the then growing steel industry of England as also for strategic considerations. On this account the various complementary and supplementary industries disappeared and those who were practising such industries fell back on the land, thereby increasing the pressure there. If we aim at relieving this pressure, we must detail off a large percentage of the population to other occupations. Further, the glamour of English education as introduced by Macaulay, drew away to towns and cities those who would have, in the ordinary course of events, supplied to the village the initiative, the imagination and the technique required in every industry. Thus the villager was left mainly with the drudge to carry on his occupation according to age-old methods.

Under the influence of capitalism, people have come to believe that price is all that matters. As the directing power under capitalism is the profit motive, all the emphasis in life is placed on money values. In our ancient organization, however, values were otherwise determined. The richest of men and princes fell at the feet of a saint. The Brahmin was at the head of all castes and not the Bania. The Kshatriya paid his homage to the savant. Even ordinarily, does a woman buy a thing just because it is the cheapest ? If a flimsy silk with a beautiful pattern is offered at a higher price along side of a coarse and durable material at a lower price, will she not choose the one with the beautiful pattern ? What is the standard of value she uses ? Not the price nor durability nor the quality of the material but the aesthetic value. At least in India, who will allow his brother and his family to starve, and with money so saved, buy finery for himself ? Does money value guide his decision or do love and duty ? We had evolved a sense of values based on human considerations and it is quite within the range of possibility to revive it in our country.

If village life is to be resuscitated, it will be imperative for men of high calibre, with the requisite initiative and imagination, to live in village and solve rural problems with the help also of modern scientific methods. This is a process which requires considerable amount of re-adjustment in our society as organized at present. Mere mechanical re-adjustment may relieve the situation immediately but no proper or lasting solution will be found unless we plan a new order based on evolution in human thought and action. More introduction of large scale machinery for example, as is used in the West, will not solve the problem. Such methods have been tried in various industries and have proved an utter failure. For instance, if instead of hand-looms we introduce power-looms for weaving saries, we are at once confronted with a variety of problems which complicate rather than remove our original difficulties. Let us assume that the power-loom is four times as efficient as the handloom so far as production goes. Let us assume also that the handloom weaver used to make about 150 saries in a year most of which would normally be marketed during the marriage season. The loom itself might cost in the neighbourhood of Rs. 75 and if the saries on an average cost about Rs. 4 each, he could carry on his trade with a small capital of about Rs. 300. The moment we introduce power-looms his production becomes 600 *saries* per year. The market does not extend four times as quickly, for we cannot, for the benefit of the weavers, have four marriage seasons in the year. The result is, that with a more or less stationary market, he requires Rs. 2,400 to produce his stuff and the loom itself would cost about Rs. 800. Instead of a capital of Rs. 300, he now requires a capital in the neighbourhood of Rs. 3,000 and even then he would have all his capital locked up until the marriage season. This situation results in competition and forced selling in order to recover his capital and capture as much of the market as he can. Usually the type of man who has been a hand-loom weaver does not possess the requisite capital and he either gets into the hands of the money-lender or has to sell out. A four fold increase of production also requires the qualities in the man to be made four times keener. Under the Western individualistic type of civilization people combine for purposes of economic activity. In our own forms of culture the combination is only for consolidating our position and safeguarding the interest of the weaker ones. Therefore it is that we often find that the methods of co-operative production as introduced by Westerners do not work in our country, the human element not being suited to them.

If in the illustration we have assumed, the situation continues as depicted, in time the hand-loom weavers will all be out of business and so will the single unit power-loom weavers and their business will drift into the hands of capitalists. The weavers will then become machine feeders or factory hands and we shall be reproducing in our country all the attendant evils of industrialized factory methods that we find in the West, culminating in war and violence.

Production and Distribution :

Besides, under capitalistic methods of production, the introduction of large scale machinery has not solved the question of unemployment. Countries like England and America which have been highly industrialized for several decades suffer actually from unemployment. Large scale machinery was a result of forced circumstances in America, where man was up against natural difficulties such as long distances, vast water courses, lofty mountains and scarcity of labour. To overcome these he had to grow, as it were, extra-hands in the forms of machinery. Therefore the function that machinery played was one of labour saving. But in our country and in all well settled countries, labour itself is the best means of distribution of wealth. If a man includes large scale machinery under his system of production, he over-weights the scale in his favour to that extent. If we look upon labour as means of distributing wealth, then we cannot have much use for the type of machinery that has been evolved by Western civilization, and which has been invented with the basic idea of exploitation and, therefore, the worker is not taken into consideration. Instead of distributing wealth, such machinery concentrates in the hands of a few. The type we need is a simple machinery, which will be within the means of the average producer in India and which will be such as will minimise drudgery and increase the efficiency of the individual but at the same time will not provide room for exploitation.

If production itself is a means of distribution of wealth then the larger the number of producers we have the more evenly will wealth be distributed. It is not conceivable that any nation can become a nation of millionaries; so, if wealth in our country is to be distributed amongst the masses, the means of production should be within the reach of all. In planning such an industrial organization, we do not aspire to produce men with income running in five and six figures, but to supply food and shelter to everybody. There is no objection to machinery as such. If there is any objection, it is to such machinery as has been devised to concentrate the profits into a few hands.

NON-VIOLENT MACHINERY

There is nothing good or evil in inanimate things. These attributes come into existence by man's reactions towards these.

A thing is good or evil according as we put it to beneficial or harmful use. Whether a contrivance is violent or non-violent depends on the purpose for which it is used. A knife used to stab a person is a violent instrument while when used to cut a fruit it is non-violent. Machines can be masters as well as servants. When used to exploit other people's labour it is the former; and when it increases the efficiency of the producer himself, it is the latter. Ordinarily, we do object to poisons being taken; but in certain cases poisons are administered as medicine. In the same way under certain restrictions and with strict control, machines are required to aid man to function better. Even the *charkha* is a machine but it does not exploit other's labour as the spinning mills do. There can be exploitation even without the use of machinery. In *Beedi* making no machines are used; yet it is an industry in which exploitation figures largely. Machine or no machine is not the fundamental question. The problem is one of finding the best way of not only supplying the material wants but also bringing employment to the people. Machinery which only saves labour is a curse in an unemployed and underemployed India, whatever it may be in other countries. Machinery can only be used to make such things as hands cannot make and where it will not displace workers gainfully employed.

Violence has used machinery to exploit others, to keep people in subjection and slavery, to destroy and murder, but non-violence can use it to help humanity to progress. We are familiar with the uses to which Western economic organization based on violence has put explosives—large scale murder and destruction of property. Explosives can be harnessed for constructive work too. Non-violent uses of it will be to blast rocks, to make tunnels, to sink wells, to work mines and quarries and even for amusements in the form of fire works.

Hence we cannot condemn explosives as a general proposition. Machinery in modern fighting forces is used for destruction. We can yoke the same power to non-violence and utilize it in the constructive sphere.

Recently, the A. I. V. I. A. decided to use machinery for paper pulp making. India has been importing about 2·5 crores worth of paper, pulp, pasteboards, etc. All this can be made by hand, but some of it is better made by machinery because the labour involved is too heavy or dangerous for men. Hence we are justified in using tools to increase our efficiency, not for exploitation. This does not put any workers out of employment; on the other hand, it will increase employment. As making of pulp from such materials as rags, bamboo, hemp etc, has never been established as an industry, the introduction of power for making such pulp cannot displace any workers of an existing industry.

There may well be sections of village industry which call for the utilization of machines as in the case of pulp making or for co-operative work as in the case of glazing and firing pottery; state power, control and aid as in the case of mining, railways, shipping, etc. Our object is, of course, to utilize human labour and provide as wide a field of employment as is possible, but this in itself may entail the use of machinery for its effective execution.

In the village movement there is a definite place for centralized industries, not for their own sakes, but as adjuncts and subsidiaries to decentralized units, just as in the political sphere a democracy does not eschew Government control and regulation when it is directed towards the better realization of individual development and expression. The village industries programme properly understood forms an exhaustive economic, social and political plan for the country as a whole.

Labour as an Entity :

In Western industrial organization, the interest of the producer himself does not figure as an end but in any system that we produce, we must keep as our central aim the welfare and the well-being of the producer and his family. In the West even where labour has evolved its own organization, the emphasis is largely on the material rather than on the human element. As against this, it must be remembered that it is not the multitude of things that we possess that makes us happy. In the "pack-type", whether under capitalism or under communism, it is thought that however soulless one's work may be, it is possible to supply this lack by devoting some time outside the factory for cultural development. Culture, of the true type, however, cannot be thus separated from our daily work. Work makes us what we are and develops the dormant qualities within us. Nothing else will enable a man to realise his true self. A man, who spends his entire life in an occupation which involves his merely carrying out the orders of others, cannot even hope to develop a sense of responsibility. Without initiative, there can be no development of personality, much less of any abiding form of culture. The system of production itself must form part of life and make life worth living. Under the centralized industrial system, production has become a nerve-racking process. We should look upon production as a continuation of the schooling of our youth. It should possess character building qualities as well as afford an education to the producer. If this can be carried out, though the material welfare of the people may not be on a par with plutocrats of the West, yet the general level of happiness will be much greater and it will produce a nation of higher average intelligence and character, which, in its turn, will be a profitable reservoir from which leaders can be drawn.

Planned economy of the Soviet pattern, on the other hand, emphasises the material production rather than the development of the individual. To enforce the plan, it is necessary to resort to violence. Such production is not natural and therefore cannot be lasting.

When power gets concentrated in the hands of a few, initiative ceases, and man is dwarfed. Such a system must lead ultimately to a form of slavery merely for the purpose of obtaining material goods.

It is commonly suggested that it is possible to afford opportunities for culture by means of providing leisure under the "pack-type" system, if the hours of work are restricted. Is this possible ? If the U.S.A. labourers can content themselves with the standard of life prevailing in India by working for two hours a day only, will they devote their leisure to cultural pursuits ? In all probability instead of doing this they will idle away their time and thus be led into demoralization and decay.

LOW PRICE OF PRODUCTS

Many wonder if the cottage methods of production can function to cheapen goods to the consumer and cite the meat-packing industry of Chicago as an instance of complete utilization of bye-products in large-scale industries which makes low prices possible.

There are three assumptions in the above question, *viz*.

(1) that complete utilization of bye-products is possible *only* in large scale industries,

(2) that large scale industries are *always* economical in the utilization of resources,

(3) that low price is an *invariable* desideratum. These we shall consider in turn.

It is true to a certain extent that large scale industries do utilize their bye-products more completely, but to make that an inseparable feature of large scale industry is wrong. A walk through our tannery at Nalwadi or the one run by Shri Satish Chandra Das Gupta at Calcutta will show the visitor that every part of a carcase, the horns, the hide, the hoofs, the fat, the flesh, the bones, the entrails, etc., can all be used even, through means within the reach of cottage units. If this is not being commonly done, the reason is the ignorance of our cottage tanners and not that such utilization is foreign to cottage units. The remedy is not to abandon cottage units but to bring the light of science to cottage workers. This is where we have failed and selfless scientists with the necessary initiative to adopt their knowledge to the simplicity of cottage resources are the desideratum and not the large scale units.

In so far as a large scale unit reduces overhead charge it is economical, but cannot be said to be the most economical utilization of our resources, especially under competitive regime, as the economic history of America can testify. Fields of cotton had to be burnt, shiploads of coffee were dumped into the sea or used as fuel, and many waste products, like molasses, rich in mineral products, are thrown out which would not be the case under cottage units. In many cases the large scale units are the most extravagant when we look at them from the national view point. Take paper-making from bamboos. No large scale unit can function unless it has a forest of bamboos at its disposal. Fresh cut bamboos have to be fed into the mill steadily. On the other hand, when we use a cottage unit, fresh cut bamboos are used for baskets, mats, granaries, roofs, etc., in the first instance; when these get rotten with use, such waste bamboos can be converted into beautiful paper. Which then is the more economic use of our resources ?

Whether low or high prices are good will depend on the cost constituents that make up the price. If the price is made up largely of cost materials, low prices are good but if such prices are made up of human labour represented by wages, then high prices will represent a better tendency to distribute wealth. When one rupee worth of mill cloth represents twelve annas worth of material, transport, interest, etc. and four annas of wages then it would be desirable to cut the items totalling twelve annas and lower the price. But when in Khadi the price is made up of twelve annas for wages and four annas for materials, cutting the price will lower the very function the industry serves in bringing happiness to mankind. Therefore, under an economy of cottage units, where labour enters largely into the composition of price, high prices are good, and under large scale industries, where labour forms a low percentage of the cost, low prices are to be aimed at.

Without a careful analysis of all those factors it would be disastrous to draw conclusions. We have to carefully scrutinise the assumptions in most of the arguments advanced in text books written for consumption in capitalistic countries, and not accept them at their face value. The danger is often great because we are fed with half truths.

Capitalism Predatory :

The gilded homes of the capitalists of Britain seem to lead people to imagine that by industrialization all poverty can be banished. Industrialization requires much capital if it is to be broad based. We can get all the needed capital for a few sugar mills or a few steel plants but that does not industrialize the country. The impetus that Britain got was predatory. But for the transfer of hoards of wealth from our land, such industrialization would have been impossible. There can be no industrialization without predation, as the needed capital cannot be accumulated out of individual effort within a life time. Britain is still at the breasts of India. If the infant is hefty, credit is due to the mother's milk. What will happen when the infant has to be weaned and has to forage for himself ? The new Russia is still a babe in the life of nations and she has her store of confiscated wealth to feed on for some centuries more. Industrialization on a national scale has not been achieved anywhere as yet. It seems an impossibility without predation and therefore, without violence.

In both capitalism and communism, then, there is room and need for violence and great concentration of power in a few hands. Because of their failure to establish a healthy equilibrium between supply and demand, we are led to advocate individual units of production rather than collective units. This adjustment in itself will reduce the excess of supplies. Markets should be localized and only the surplus, after satisfying local needs, ought to find distant markets.

The present economic system reminds one of old time steamers which could be sunk by springing one hole in the hull, but modern steamers have watertight compartments which prevent the ship from sinking, even if a part is damaged. Similarly, when overproduction and the market are not centralized, the dangers of the system, as a whole coming to grief, are few. In such a decentralized system the danger of violence too is greatly minimised.

Centralization :

We must of course, have a place for centralized production but it must be only for the purposes of public utilities which should be under either collective or co-operative control. Undertakings such as telephones, telegraphs, roads, postal services, supply of water, exploitation of forests and mines will all naturally come within the scope of the State. We cannot allow private exploitation in these undertakings. The main objection to social ownership and management for commodity production is that under such conditions progress will be retarted. But if social control can take care of the size and capacity of the units of production exploitation can be minimised. As long as human nature is what it is, it will be impracticable to abolish exploitation altogether. Exploitation and violence in some form or other will be there. Our eating and breathing is full of violence and exploitation. Our purpose, however, should be to minimise these in keeping with human existence and progress. Under the conditions we propose there will be a natural limit to the capacity of an individual to produce. And this, in its turn, will limit maldistribution of wealth. So long as individuals differ one from another, the quantity and the quality of production of the individual will also differ. That is, the income will differ, but the range of difference will be limited. We can think of differences in annual income ranging in hundreds but we cannot have incomes running into millions without involving an unhampered exploitation of thousands. Finance, trading, marketing etc., can also function in a co-operatively managed organization and, threfore, there need be no fear of unlimited private wealth.

Under the form of State control which we advocate, the transition may not be sudden and spectacular, our methods will be slow and will take time to permeate through the nation. We have to have patience if we are aiming at permanence. While disestablishing private property by a stroke of the pen by legislation may be violent, gradual curtailment of private ownership by limiting productive capacity under state control will not necessarily spell violence. In our own country, in the past as well as in the present, a great many functions were and still are under social control and society decides on the merits or demerits of certain cases. There may be abuses in this system, but it does indicate the possibility of subjecting our people to group discipline by social control.

CHAPTER 12 NON-VIOLENT STANDARD OF LIFE

STANDARD FIXED BY WANTS

Economists in industrialized countries hold that if the standard of living is raised then the incentive to produce more is greater and this will ultimately enhance the income. Within certain limits this is perfectly true. Raising the standard of living means increasing the wants of the people. The older generation may have eaten with their fingers, on leaves and then thrown the leaves to feed the goats, which give them milk. The next generation is taught to eat at table with forks, spoons and plates and have servants to wait on them and wash the dishes. In time we get a generation which cannot eat without these man-made accessories. This places tables, chairs, forks, spoons, plates, dishes and servants on the list of necessities and also creates an inelastic demand for the goods of the manufacturers of these articles. It is open to question whether the new mode of life is any cleaner, happier, and conducive to human progress than the older methods. Yet it is good for business as the later generations will work hard to get these articles rather than go without them. Alongside of this increase of wants they set up a social scale of ostentatious living which insures against reversion to old customs through sheer pride. By this means people are whipped into activity by the gnawing inside caused by artificial wants. Industrialists cash in these urges by pace setters in factories who make the workers function at the highest pitch of efficiency. There is no doubt that this will increase the income of the workers. But what do they do with this hard earned income? They buy anything from anywhere, without discrimination, as long as the material goods they acquire satisfy their artificially acquired demand. This leads to self-indulgence and self-gratification as a principle of life. We get an eternal struggle for more and more with an ever receding scale of wants leaving the people always discontented. Often even at the cost of necessities luxuries are emphasised to make an impression on others. Persons, who are victims of this scheme of increasing the income by raised standards of living, are on a par with the donkey before which its driver has dangled a much coveted carrot hanging from a stick fixed to its own harness. The more the animal runs to get at the carrot, the further is the cart down. The driver gets his work done and the carrot remains. Under this scheme the industrialists get the goods made and sold but the life of the people is not enriched. The powerful *modus operandi* employed is to influence the psychology of the people by well devised advertisements and to control the system of educatin of the young. This is the way of violence and exploitation and it is largely applicable in industrialized countries where it creates wide and increasing demand for manufactured articles.

STANDARD FIXED BY INCOME

Instead of fixing the standard of living by raising wants we may allow income to fix its own standard giving due weight to the individual's tastes as to what the wants uninfluenced by what standard he is expected by society to live up to. This is the more natural way and hence allows expression of personality of the consumer. You may judge the character of a persons by the items on his budget.

In our country the majority of the people are undernourished. Therefore cosiderable volume of increased income will be absorbed by the item "diet" in the first stages. Being an agricultural country our attention is to be directed to food growing and allied village industries supplying primary needs. This explains why the A. I. V. I. A. has taken up as its first line of attack improving of industries like flour grinding, paddy husking, oil pressing, gur making etc.

The average per capita income in villages is in the neighbourhood of Rs. 15/- per year *i.e.*, a family income of Rs. 7/- or Rs. 8/- per month. A fairly balanced diet for one person will cost that much. Hence there can be no sense in talking of increasing the standard of living in terms of manufactured goods in India until we increase the present income by more than seven to eight times when alone the basic animal needs of food will be satisfied.

SCALES OF INCOME

In any country standards of income have to have a direct bearing to the income derived by the masses of the people from the basic occupation. In our country our scale has to be based on agriculture from which precarious occupation even Rs. 10/- per month is hard to obtain. Diligent and skillful artisans may secure Rs. 30-40/ and under abnormal condition may even get double that amount. These incomes in villages are gains from their own labour and include hardly any item of exploitation. Calculating on this scale the A.I. V. I. A. is working on a maximum scale of salaries for its workers of Rs. 75/- per month. Anything much above that will be diverging too far from the condition of the people we profess to serve. Even this is based on the more rosy side of rural life and is only enjoyed by the best of villagers.

If our incomes are interdependent it becomes imperative that we count the effect which our purchases will have on the income of our neighbours. We become discriminating buyers and will naturally be interested in buying the products of our neighbours. This instills self-discipline and develops self-control and is partly a fulfilment of our trsuteeship of wealth.

FALSE SCALES

Unfortunately in our country, standards of living have been set up by an alien people intent on exploitation. In John Company's days the servants of the company had to be paid large enough salaries to keep them from bribery and corruption and the scale itself was related to the vast profits of merchants and marauders who stalked the land and this easy and quick method of acquiring a fortune presented an alternative line of employment to the servants of the company. Hence it is we find in a poor country like ours a scale of pay for Government servants before which even the pensions allowed to ancient ruling families pale into insignificance. The effect of this foreign plunder standard of salaries has found its repercussions in all emoluments including those of professions. If the district official gets Rs. 2500/- p.m. the leading practitioner at the bar has to aim at that figure if he is to maintain that standard and move in that circle. So also the medical practitioner. This immediately sets the false standard in motion. The salaries of the teachers have to be high enough to enable them to call in the surgeon and pay him Rs. 15/- per visit and so on. This whole scale is foreign to us and has no bearing on the conditions prevailing in the country. The presence of this false scale does create a tremendous difficulty to those of us in the transitional stage. A worker who gets

Rs. 75/- per month cannot afford to get the best medical aid although he has a "princely" income on the village indigenous scale. But once the whole country follows the latter scale and the pirates scale is thrown overboard even the best of physicians will be content with four annas a visit and law will be administered free. Motilal Nehrus, Bhulabhai Desais and Saprus will forsake their tens of thousands and be content to give the benefit of their fertile brains for an income of about Rs. 100/- per month. This is the standard we have to work towards if we would have a *non-violent standard of life*. When we attain this even a man with Rs. 75/- per month will get as much real income as a man with Rs. 1000/- p.m. to-day, as the advice of a physicians who charges Rs. 15/- per visit to-day will be just as valuable even when he charges only four annas per visit. The maldistribution of wealth we find to-day will disappear and there will be equality of standard of life throughout the nation.

CHAPTER 13 BARTER EXCHANGE

With the progress of civilization, division of labour becomes inevitable, but there is a limit beyond which, if it is carried, it will lead to deterioration and inefficiency. The throat specialist, who ignores the human constitution behind it and deals with one organ alone without taking into consideration the whole body, visualises a monster, and is bound to be a failure. We cannot let division of labour be carried to an extreme, forgetting the setting and the personality of the worker. Even within such limits, division of labour calls for an exchange of goods. Such exchange can only be healthy if it results in mutual benefit. That is the basis of all legitimate trade.

Exchange as an End :

In the simplest form goods exchange for goods. A producer-consumer meets a consumer-producer; that is barter. As the market expands and trade advances in complexity, there arises a need for a medium to facilitate this exchange. This brought into being tokens, or other commodities or a standard metal as media and ultimately resulted in the money economy we are labouring under. Exchange itself has now become a source of profit. The means has been turned into an end by the present form of money.

Exchange as a Means :

Money exchange is indispensable mainly for the extension of markets. Money in itself satisfies no want except that of a miser who delights in counting his coins. It is a temporary storage of purchasing power and a convenient standard of value. When a person wants to sell his cow and get a wireless set it may not be possible for him to find one and the same exchange. Therefore money intervenes and enables the seller to dispose off his cow first to anyone who wants a cow, and store the purchasing power represented by the value of the cow in the form of money till he meets one who has wireless sets to sell, and than he exchanges that purchasing power for the radio set. This medium becomes all the more essential when great distances separate the market for the cow from the market for the radio sets. Under modern imperialism where one country is kept down to produce raw materials for another distant country which produces manufactured articles, money economy has become the life breath of commerce. Although international settlements may be in goods, customers cannot buy an American motor car against the delivery of stacks of straw.

Extension of markets in their turn call for the Army, Navy and the Air Force to control them in the interests of particular nations. Money and credit have their place in commerce and trade. Though theirs is an important role, yet they have to be reined in and bridled if their functioning is to bring the people nothing but good in their wake. A properly balanced exchange economy, calculated to curb these tendencies, must provide for an element of barter. Inflation of currency during war time by the use of postage stamps, matches and playing cards as money must not be mistaken for barter which alone can help to retard the evil effects of money.

Where the standard of living of a people is near the subsistence level their purchasing power is spent mostly on food and other necessities. At such a stage, if money is largely used, then it would divert that purchasing power to some extent into luxuries, which often come from distant countries, and thus lower the true wealth computed in terms of human values. When money is taken by Government from a petty farmer, to whom it may mean so many day's food, and is paid to a high salaried official, to whom the same amount may mean the price of a cigar, money exchange is the means of obliterating human values in wealth, and causing an avoidable loss in national wealth. This is especially noticeable in Governmental transactions, which under such circumstances become the means of impoverishing the people. A barter system would have helped to make it impossible for Government to perpetrate the injustice of using India's reserves to the tune of crores in the London money market while our industries were starving for funds.

On the other hand, the use of barter in collecting taxes from the poor and disbursing it in kind lessens the chances of national waste and to a large extent acts as a check on Government waste. Such a system of tax collection and disbursement, of course, involves a great deal of administrative and organizational difficulties but none that is insurmountable. To avoid inconveniences modern centralized Governments have thrown overboard admirable financial systems like the ones advocated by the Islamic and Jewish Codes of payment of taxes in kind by way of tithes, *i. e.* one-tenth of whatever is produced.

Though these systems are rare today, we see them still functioning with great efficiency in some Islamic States as in the Pathan States of Swat, Dir and Chitral on the Frontier. The State employs contractors to collect the State share of the actual produce—not estimated values in terms of money prices as in British India. The State share is generally one-tenth of all produce. In the case of sheep etc., the due is one animal for every completed 40 in the flock, with the option of payment of an equivalent in ghee or other animal produce. For cattle the owner has to give one seer of ghee per annum for keeping the herd and grazing fees are paid by contract to the landlords.

There are Government contractors who act as bankers for these payments in kind. They receive the share of produce due to the State, store them and disburse them as directed by the State. They carry on external trade in the surplus of the produce and pay into the treasury the cash realised. They also control a great proportion of the internal trade. This readily places at the disposal of the Government an effective instrument to control prices at definite and convenient points of focus. Government employees—military and civil—below the rank of gazetted officers are paid once every six months partly in cash, while the higher officers draw their pay in cash from the treasury.

This system will enable us to get over many a handicap from which the farmer in British India suffers. Under the present system of collecting taxes in money the farmer is forced to sell his crops, sometimes even before harvesting, to find the wherewithal to satisfy the Revenue Department. Apart from the evils already dealt with in the earlier paragraphs, the effect on the market of such forced premature sales is to depress prices and burden the farmers with further losses.

If the periodical payments in kind to Government servants were so scheduled as to synchronise with the harvesting of wheat, rice, juwar, bajri, maize, cotton, etc., the difficulties of storage would be minimised, and such payments, though they may affect the import of manufactured goods adversely which will be unpalatable to foreign interests, would ensure an adequate distribution of food grains within the country and save the middlemen's charges to some extent.

An efficient exchange should facilitate proper distribution among the people. The modern problem is not one of production but of distribution. People are in dire need. The producers can produce large supplies, but the people are not able to make their wants effective for lack of purchasing power. A boy stands before a sweet-meat shop with his mouth watering for the goods displayed in the window, but his pocket is empty. His demand for the sweets is ineffective. Under the money economy he should have a mint at his disposal to enable him to obtain what he wants, or he will have to beg, borrow or steal purchasing power.

The way to non-violent control of the market, to a distribution of wealth with the minimum of friction, and to a mint under the control of the people is pointed out by Gandhiji in his proposal that a warp length of a single thread of yarn be taken as the lowest measure of value by Khadi lovers. If this mint comes into vogue, the boy standing in front of the sweet-meat shop need only go home, take up his takali and spin the required length of yarn to get his coveted sweet-meat. The people will have a mint at their disposal. This mint will neither debase the coin nor will it inflate the corrency. It will neither need the Army, Navy and the Air Force for its control, nor will call in the Police for its protection.

In our country which abounds in labour wealth and suffers from a lack of opportunities for profitable employment but has an unlimited market for necessaries, this device is calculated to give a hallmark to things that are running waste today and bring to them into the market as coveted commodities.

Metal coins which have a commodity value in themselves are imperishable, while consumable goods, for which they are used as substitutes in the process of exchange depreciate with time. A seller of plantains has not the same bargaining power as the metal owner. The plantains will soon rot and so he has to come to terms quickly. But the money owner can afford to wait as he can hold on to money any length of time. Hence the power of bargaining rests with the possessor of the imperishable metal coins. Thus the seller labours under a disadvantage. This is turned into profit by the money owner. Herein is the incentive to hoard which naturally restricts consumption and thereby the circulation of money.

With a tendency to fall in price levels over a period of time, metal money is an increasing burden to the debtor and growing wealth to the creditor. Thus it accentuates the existing inequality in the distribution of wealth.

Disparity between Production & Consumption :

In addition to these inherent defects, the centralized methods of production which call for highly expensive equipment have also shut off money from circulation. The pay roll of production is not sufficient to buy goods produced for consumption as part of the purchasing power is kept back to provide capital renewals and reserves. This is one of the main reasons for the present depression in the world. If the economic life of a people is to flow like a river that gathers strength as it flows, it is necessary that a great deal of facilities for consumption of goods produced have to be provided. This can be done only by releasing purchasing power and not by restricting it. On the shores of a fresh water lake of plenty, humanity is standig parched with thirst for the lack of a golden cup to drink out of. Under the capitalistic regime we have been taught not to approach the water without a golden cup in hand, and we have accepted the situation as the only possible way of quenching our thirst.

The present system is designed to satisfy only what is called by economists "the effective demand"—that is the man with the golden cup—and not the natural demand—that is the man with the parched throat.

Employment Cornered :

To make matters worse, the credit facilities extended by banking organizations make more purchasing power available to production while consumption is starved further. By the clever designing of money economy the capitalist—the money monopolist—has cornered all the work available. He doles them out to the wage slaves. More and more, all industries are rapidly passing under financial control. Centralized methods of production call for heavy expense in plant and machinery and he who is able to control such equipment controls the right to give employment.

Money economy makes it easy to shift purchasing power from one place to another readily. A centralized Government, like the Government of India, is always tempted to spend its revenues in towns and cities; thus it draws its revenues from villages and its expenditure enriches towns. The State also controls the quantity of money without an efficient check on the prices. All these go to make the poor man poorer and the rich man richer.

Effect on Villages :

As our land is a land of villages, we have to see what effect such monetary system has on our farmers. When villagers exchange goods locally, the wealth of the village remains unaffected. Also, when the villager exchanges goods in the neighbourhood, there is no loss of wealth. But when the villages have to transfer their purchasing power for "services" which are never tendered nor for which there is any need, they become poor progressively. The farmer's voice is inaudible in the councils of the nation. He has no control over the spending of the purchasing power he transfers to the Government. Similarly, when he buys goods from foreign countries, there is no guarantee he gets a square deal. The frontiers are studded with hurdles he has to leap, and as he is not accustomed to these feats, he falls a prey to the better equipped. Farmers are as a rule in debt and money economy increases such burdens with fall in prices. He has many pitfalls. The human tendency to gamble is exploited by middlemen by introducing money crops which are fatally speculative to those who have no reserves. In time they are reduced to the position of slaves to supply raw material to factories owned by capitalists. They surrender their freedom for a little higher price and ultimately ruin themselves by going in for such crops instead of growing food and other materials for their own local industries.

In Malabar the former rice lands have been converted into coconut groves and these coconut groves are producing coconuts, not for human consumption, but for oil for soap mills. Is producing "Lux" soap, in however large a quantity, an increase of production when this is done at the cost of people's staple food ? The people who were formerly cultivating rice are at present being given polished rice imported from Brazil. Hence, in the final analysis, the mill owners' efforts have resulted in the provision of Brazilian polished rice to the people who were once eating wholesome, unpolished rice of their own production and converted these rice lands into raw material suppliers for soap making.

With the help of money economy, these things are done without the victim being aware of it. Money is not a safe method of valuing articles, especially of primary necessities. For instance, at Avanashi firka a good deal of the milk produced was being sent to Coimbatore. The value of a pound of milk is in the nutrition it affords. The milk producer, if he gives it to his child, ensures sufficient calcium to build up the child's bones, fat and other nutritious materials to build up the body. The value of the milk from the nutritional point of view is the same whether it is consumed by the mill owner or the producer's child. We may even say the value of milk is greater when given to a growing child than when given to an adult. Just because the rich mill-owner of Coimbatore is able to offer As. 8/- for a pound of milk, the Avanashi producer deprives his child of this nutritious food, and sends it away to Coimbatore. In so doing he does not realise that he is, in effect, selling the future health of the child.

Sometime ago the paper carried the news that Rs. 27/- lakhs worth of sugarcane was to be destroyed in U. P. as the factories were not prepared to crush them and the farmers were unable to dispose of them due to difficulties created by human agency.

Again, taxes which are to be paid in money take away a certain and definite quantity out of a very uncertain production. If the Government accept their dues in kind, it will be beneficial to the farmers and villagers in many ways. High pressure salesmanship and the artful ways of modern marketing methods make the farmer part with his purchasing power for that which does not satisfy his wants. They buy cheap foreign-made goods to their own detriment and unemployment. Buying from distant markets without a free flow back from that market brings impoverishment and unemployment ultimately to the buyer himself. Therefore, we have to restrict our buying to nearby producing centres until such time when there is fluidity in the market. To day, talking of an international market, while discriminating freight rates, customs duties, national control of currencies and such like barriers are rampant, is an absurdity. It is usually done to capture the unwary. So let us beware and deal in nothing but locally produced goods.

True Value and Motives :

All values of commodities depend on the productive capacity of the people ultimately. Social need should be the criterion of value. At present, by our process of education, we have been taught to value everything from the point of view of money. Human values have been lost sight of. Labour itself is paid for as a commodity, not as a producer, and social status attaches to one who labours least but controls much purchasing power. Under a proper standard of valuation, status in society should attach to service to community. This wrong emphasis supplies a social motive for accumulation of wealth and results in a money monopoly and curbing of other people's liberty. With the piling up of huge fortunes, it has been necessary to find outlets by international investments which culminate in wars. Finacial capitalism has ushered in this epoch of international moneylending. As long as this continues, we shall look in vain for peace. As long as society attaches a position of honour to one who controls purchasing power, the incentive to consume is curbed and ultimately leads to overproduction and economic depression.

Money and War :

Production under money economy ignores social values and follows lines where largest profits are to be made. Thus it is that we find the best brains engaged not in devising ways and means of supplying the needs of the people, but how one nation may hold another in subjection by the most modern methods of destruction. Intensive research is directed into the field of atom bombs and other insidious methods of wholesale massacre. The mechanism of price is yoked on the exploitation. Production follows pecuniary gains and makes no effort to study the needs of the people. We find in our own country the supply of necessities has made place for curio trades putting many out of employment. Foreign trade is held up as the acme of civilization and a thing to strive for at all costs. To do all this damage effectively, it was essential to mount the golden calf on a high pedestal. The natural ratio of exchange between countries should be determined by the internal purchasing power of their respective currencies, and not by any other means. This has been proved beyond question since the dethroning of the gold standard in practice.

Conclusion :

What then is our conclusion ? We find that a great many evils and pitfalls await us if we blindly follow the yellow metal. We have to correlate the perishability of the consumable goods with the medium of exchange if we are to place both the buyer and the seller on an equal footing and encourage consumption. Encouraging consumption rather than hoarding will lead to better distribution of wealth. To do so, our ideas of values will have to be educated and re-oriented from the standpoint of human progress as against individual profit. We have to restrict our markets to a great extent and avoid buying from distant places.

To give effect to the spirit of barter it is not necessary for us to wait till our monetary system has been reformed. The basic principle of barter is to reduce the chain of exchange and bring the producer and consumer together. Money economy has elongated the chain by forging several links between the producer and the consumer. We can effectively shorten the distance by supporting local industries. The smaller the circle the nearer to barter do we approximate and we ensure that the whole benefit of economic activity will rest with the community which produces and consumes. When we thus restrict our transactions to the locality, though we may be using coins, we shall be virtually basing our exchange on barter.

Too much planning in production surrenders the individual interests to an oligarchy. Today the problem is to direct consumption. In the course of the last century we have seen that production is capable of taking good care of itself.

Equality among nations can only be attained with economic independence. Inequality leads to war. What the propagandists call "Internationalism" is really a misnomer for "Supernationalism". It is such a supernationalism that the nations of Europe are striving for. Each wishes to be that supreme supernational. Hence the war preparation at a feverish heat that we witness. We can have no peace until this epoch of international lending is brought to an end and each nation restricts itself to its home markets. Money economy has carried us beyond our depths and extended the markets beyond control. Barter provides a ready means of restraining any tendency to run amuck.

CHAPTER 14 ECONOMIC SURVEYING AND PLANNING

Different Types :

Surveys and Plans are not all of one kind. They differ widely. For the sake of convenience we may divide them into four groups (a) Academic, (b) Propagandic, (c) Clinical and (d) Diagnostic.

Academic Surveys :

Persons who enter upon an academic survey, however well they may be equipped otherwise, are supposed to approach it not with an open mind but with a blank mind. Every thing has to be proved to the hilt, the evidence being based on statistics, authoritative statements and other well-documented propositions. Finance and cost of the enquiry are no consideration. Eternity is the time limit for perfection. Scientific accuracy is the sole aim. The outlook has to be detached and dispassionate and no personal contact with the problem is needed. The results are left in the lap of God.

It will be imperative to marshal volumes of statistics to prove that the villagers are poor. Labourious enquiries will have to be made to be convinced that the villagers are starving. Unearthing of long forgotten historical documents will be needed to establish that the industries are languishing. Beautifully written volumes will record these findings.

Such have been the innumerable reports of various Royal Commissions and Governmental enquiries. Judged by their results they have been perfectly futile. They cannot be otherwise. Experts are brought from distant lands to ensure the condition that they come with a blank mind. They have no contact with the people. They seek none. They move in an artificial atmosphere and finally help to fill the many pigeonholes in the Secretariat with their pious propositions and lengthy resolutions.

Propagandic Surveys :

When certain desired ends have to be attained it is imperative that the public should be led towards the set goal by skillfully managed Keddah operations. Just as elephants are driven to the trap by closing all possible exist by cleverly planned beating and manoeuvring, the unsuspecting person is told what he should think by means of adept reasoning with manipulated statistics and half-truths. Here the persons on the Committee do not come to the work with a blank mind, but with a packed mind or a prejudice to fulfil a set purpose. Such are propagandic surveys.

In this method as in the former, elaborate procedure has to be gone through to distract the victim much in the same way as the magician directs the attention of his audience to irrelevant matters before he performs his sleight of hand-tricks.

Surveys of this type are undertaken by imperialist economists like J. M. Keynes or Government Protagonists like M. L. Darling or F. L. Brayne. These reports may not be as innocuous as the former but may result in actual injury as in the case of the exchange ratio.

Clinical Surveys :

In the clinical survey the purpose is to obtain knowledge or experience. When the surgeon is lecturing, his concern is not the recovery of the patient but the study of the malady. The patient is a mere detail and presents a convenient medium to focus attention on the disease. The persons engaged in such surveys are either pedants wishing to produce learned books or students in Universities working for the hall-mark of degrees. A survey of this nature may be undertaken without any regard to utility.

There may be no field work, the library being the sole source of information with such other facts as a well-drafted questionnaire may elicit.

No material results are expected or planned for. Our libraries are stocked full of such tomes clarifying definition and rehashing ideas. These works are still born and are of no utilitarian value.

Diagnostic Surveys :

The Diagnostic Survey centres its attention not on the disease but on the patient. The doctor does not approach the sick bed with a blank mind, or with a prejudice, or with the desire to vivisect his patient with a view to furthering his knowledge, but proceeds to apply his well-trained and richly stocked brain to the problem of restoring the sick-man to health and strength. It is an application of previously obtained experience to the present situation. All enquiries are directed towards that end. The reaction of the enquirer to the immediate subject is of the essence. The efforts are not directed towards writing a book on tuberculosis, nor towards warning all and sundry against this fell disease, nor in acquiring further knowledge, but to save the patient.

This attitude colours the whole procedure. It is presumed that the physician knows all about the disease. It is not necessary for him to prove that such a disease exists and that human beings are susceptible to it and so on. We assume he knows all that. His purpose is to find a quick remedy. Time and cost are primary considerations, and the diagnosis and the remedy should be closely connected with the patient. The doctor will be judged by the results he produces. In the personality of the Surveyor many things are taken for granted and what is looked for is his reaction to the situation. It is true questions have to be asked, the temperature has to be taken but they are all directed towards an end.

The methods followed by Gandhiji are good examples of surveys of this type. Without much sophisticated trumpet-blowings and pedantic procedures he is able to place his finger on the spot and suggest remedies.

We shall now proceed to consider the requisites of this method of work as regards the personnel, procedure and plan.

Personnel :

Just as it would be absurd for a medical man to set out to diagnose a case without having had an intensive training and a period of preparation, no one should have the audacity to start a survey or suggest a plan without having had a thorough preparation for it. We would laugh a person to scorn if after being called to attend on a sick-man he proceeds to the Medical College to learn the A. B. C. of the matter. Yet many a committee is brought into being under such utterly ridiculous conditions—men who are total strangers to the land and to the people are put on it. Unfortunately even many professors of Economics have no living touch with the people. They may be able to repeat the reports of the Royal Commissions backwards and discuss at great length fine points of economic theory but that is no qualification so long as they live far from the real India. We do not need ornamental heads or a galaxy of magnates of Finance, Science, Economics and other departments of life but we must have men devoted to the cause. What is the cause ? If they come with due preparation, there will be no need to prove the basic conditions in the country. If they know them, there can be only one course *viz.* the amelioration of the economic condition of the people. With this as the primary objective the procedure will be selected to serve the desired end.

If the work is entrusted to a Committee, every member of the Committee should contribute his quota. There is no status attached to membership of such a Committee other than what service rendered will bring and no self-interest can be sought in it. Therefore it should be a Committee of devoted workers.

Financial :

Ours is a poor country and it will be an irony of fate if those entrusted with the preparation of a plan to relieve poverty started by accentuating it. The human value of wealth is reduced when transferred from the poor man to the rich man. Generally such survey committees are drawn from the comparatively well-to-do or rich classes. And if the expenses of commission are met from taxation, which is drawn from the poor, there is a loss of national wealth. Therefore, such committees should not draw anything more than actuals and even such actuals should be of the minimum. These undertakings are not money-making ventures. Even officials who may be detailed off on such duties should realise the contradiction involved in drawing fat salaries and allowances when engaged on such work. For the same reason the period of work must be curtailed and made as short as possible.

Procedure :

The same consideration will call for a simple procedure. All work not material to the purpose should be avoided. There should be no need for an elaborate questionnaire unless the problem is approached with a blank mind. The questionnaire should be like the pointed questions a medical man asks his patient to know the immediate disturbing causes and the symptoms, and they should be as few as possible so as not to cause an undue strain on the patient.

The members of the Committee must come into close contact with those whose condition the Committee seeks to improve. For this they may have to visit villages and obtain first hand information. If the Committee takes it duties seriously this contact will be fundamental to its work because it is the focus from which everything will radiate. Without such a starting point there will be no meaning to its work. If for instance, we talk of "Key Industries" what are key industries is a question that naturally arises. To which treasure-house is this a key ? If we are striving to uplift the masses then the treasure-house is the means of affording gainful occupation to the masses and key industries are those which are elemental to the industries followed by the masses. It is the approach that givs content to the words commonly used. As we presume that members enter on their duties with due preparation there will be no need to make an exhaustive survey of facts. A few well-chosen areas or groups should be studied carefully to get at the real maladies of the masses. This sampling will also considerably curtail the time and the expense. Many things are done on the basis of information gathered from experience and not with the aid of an exhaustive enquiry. If a train has to be sent from Bombay to Calcutta we do not first gather information about the exact number of 1st, 2nd and 3rd class passengers with their luggage calculated to the ounce at every station enroute both of alighting passengers and those who are to board the train. If we tried to proceed on this method, not a single train could run. And yet some of the Royal Commissions have thought this was the proper way to go about their business and hence they have been futile. There is a strong tendency amongst us to copy this seemingly scientific method. Let us beware of its laudable plausibility.

Planning :

Having obtained the necessary reactions, information and facts we should proceed to plan. The whole scheme should be practicable and not ask for the moon. The first steps should be well defined keeping in mind the immediate wants of the masses. If the committee has an ideal that ideal will be reflected in its plan. For instance, the Congress has repeatedly set before itself the ideal of working for the welfare of the masses. So any plan emanating from a Congress Committee should be mass-centred *i. e.*, the approach will be to co-ordinate the economic plan so as to enable the masses to strengthen their economic position. As already pointed out key industries will be organized to serve their needs. Public utilities and natural resources will not be allowed to be exploited for private profit but must be run on a service basis. If India is to organize herself on the basis of non-violence there can be no other way.

Every industry has to be studied with care and the component processes analysed to find out the proper parties on whom the different functions should fall. For instance, a careful analysis will show that in transforming hides into leather there are many processes, some demanding the attention of individuals and others falling to the lot of Government. The carcass has to be flayed and the hide should be salted immediately. Any delay in salting will allow putrefaction to set in. A putrefied skin cannot make good leather. Even if the carcass is dragged about the hide will be damaged irreparably; the value of the hide will go down in much greater proportion to the apparent damage. Time is a factor in tanning. *Chamars* are members of a community that is weak financially and as at present organized, the whole burden falls on them with the result that tanning is not given sufficient time. Our leather is bad and possible national wealth is thrown away. Hides should be considered a national wealth and anything that lessens the value of it should therefore command the attention of the State. When properly planned, Government should shoulder the responsibility for supervising flaying and as salt is a monopoly, should supply salt duty-free to preserve the hide and secure access to cheap tanning material and protect the industry from outside competition and relieve the *Chamars* from financial strain. Thus the various factors of production are co-ordinated and divided between the State and the people each functioning in the processes it is best fitted to perform. This is planning. Without such functional distribution of productive operations there can be no planning. The formal control of the State is a pre-requisite to such planning.

In the absence of such popular control over the State the All-India Spinners' Association and the All-India Village Industries Association have stepped in to the place and have been striving to supply the State functions of organization finance, standardization, marketing, research, industrial education and dissemination of information to the extent to which private effort without legislative power can do. Even the protection that should have been given by law, has been given to a limited extent by these Associations by harnessing Patriotism and Public Opinion to this end.

Working under a Planned Economy is like working in a laboratory—under an artificially made environment which can be readily altered to suit changing conditions. Therefore, a nation-wide effective Planning demands complete independence having control over Finance, the Military and the Railways. Without such powers, to plan is merely to play with the problems.

CHAPTER 15 PLANNED ECONOMY

While planned Economy is an innovation to the Occident brought to the fore largely by Soviet Russia, the dust of ages has settled on the planned orders of the Orient. The whole of the Indian social order is a planned economy that has been functioning for thousands of years. That it should have served us so well all these many centuries is a monument to the farsightedness of the conceivers and to the soundness of the eternal principles upon which it was based. The Hindu order covers all phases of life—political, social, religious and economic, while the Russian experiment is confined mainly to the economic sphere. The inauguration of the Russian plan is child's play when compared with the stupendous difficulties of communications in the days of yore when the many-sided Hindu plan was launched over a vast country like India.

The Objective :

Planning connotes a definite objective towards the attainment of which we direct all activities of the nation. Therefore it is imperative that we should have our goal clearly before us. In the Russian experiment, because of the background of the Czarist regime, the goal set was the material well-being of a certain class. All other considerations were subordinate to this one idea—living in plenty like the old aristocrats.

In our country we have a double background—a philosophy of non-violence, on which the old plan was based and the bondage of British Imperialism. As a resultant of these two factors, we find Gandhiji battling for freedom through non-violent means. Freedom for the individual means freedom to do what is right, to think for himself and express his thoughts, and to work for himself as and how he likes. In human society, freedom is not a license to act in any way one wishes; it implies duties, rights and limitations. Our rights are curbed by our duties to others. When the curbing is done by an external force we have a society based on violence depending on the army, navy, air-force and the police. But when the curbing is from within, we have a society based on non-violence and the sense of one's duty towards one's neighbours.

In a society based on violence there is really not much freedom. The *lathi* is held over the head of the citizen if he fails to obey the mandates of a central authority. Such obedience as is obtained through this means is the outcome of fear which ultimately leads to hatred and suspicion. In the modern highly organized States, like Germany, and Italy, citizenship is a form of slavery—slavery not to individual owners but to a glorified State. Instead of the State being an instrument to serve the people, the people are imprest into the service of the State. True freedom cannot thrive in an atmosphere of fear, hatred and suspicion.

True freedom should be conducive to the growth of the people. Under it man will become less of a beast and more human, less selfish and more social, less violent and more dutiful, less materialistic and more humane. This indeed is a test of true freedom. Any organization, which depends on the regimentation of the people, hampers their growth and retards their evolution. However attractive the immediate effects of hot-house growth may seem, it is at best unnatural and will vanish the moment the artificial environment is removed. of we want the genuine article we shall have to have the patience to allow it to evolve in its own good time. Violent methods may produce results quickly but such results are not lasting, they are ephemeral. India has a foundation laid through centuries for the building up of a non-violent society. If we rebuild our society on this foundation, our civilization will be real. It is to be regretted that a civilization similar to ours in Japan has been abandoned in favour of a flashy cultivated barbarity. Do we want to go that way ? Or, shall we proceed to find the freedom that Tagore visualised in the following lines ?

"Where the mind is without fear
And the head is held high,
Where knowledge is free;
Where the world has not been broken up into
fragments by narrow domestic walls.

Where words come out from the depth of truth;
Where tireless striving stretches its arms towards perfection;
Where the clear stream of reason has not lost its
way into the dreary desert sand of dead habit;

Where the mind is led forward by thee into ever-widening
thought and action—
Into that heaven of freedom, my father,
let my country awake."

The Means :

How shall we attain the above objective ? In the previous paragraph we have considered that our goal should be the emancipation of the individual in a non-violent society.

The people have a certain background of non-violent culture behind them and we have to find the means of developing them further. Violent methods are precluded to us. Hence we have to use cultural means to develop the individual. Self-discipline and self-control are the pivots on which such a society can work. We have, therefore, to devise such methods as will be conducive to this end. These qualities cannot be attained without much effort. People have to be drilled into them. Instruments, like the radio and cinema, however efficient they may be as means of propaganda and amusement, will fail us in developing culture which, to achieve the best results, demands that the subject must actively co-operate with the instrument and not play merely a passive part. A musician cannot be produced by making him listen into the best of music on the radio. The subject has to battle with his instrument for years and years before he can appear before the public as a good musician. Superficial experience and knowledge do not produce culture; it comes only with the permeation of experience into the subconscious self. It takes time, it takes trouble; but it is lasting and worth all the effort. If the nation is to have a non-violent culture or civilization, it would involve considerable conscious effort.

In an imperialism evolved out of piracy, it has been necessary to glorify the men trained in the art of violence by giving them the highest status in society. In a non-violent society we have renounced violence and all property, and have dedicated ourselves to service. We have to produce a cultural standard based on eternal values. Money values can be of little help when our struggle is to rise above the material world of selfishness and ostentation. We must guard against the great temptation of mistaking the means for the end.

If we obtain political independence and we are left without the ability to use it for the benefit of the people, such independence will be meaningless to us. If to maintain such independence we have to keep up large forces under arms, we shall be not depriving the freedom of th e persons in the fighting units but defeating our own purpose. Hence, we have to scrutinise the choice of the means very carefully.

GOVERNMENT

The aim of politics is to serve the masses. By political means we get control of Government and use Government functions to serve the needs of the people. In the matters of State there are many things that call for a long view of affairs, which are naturally opposed to short-sighted interests often governing the decisions of individuals. Therefore, such items which have to be undertaken in the common interests of the nation, though in some cases these may be directly opposed to individual interests, have to be detailed out to a group of men who can be relied on to do their duty by the nation as a whole.

The members of this group will not attempt to exploit their position; they will be paid an allowance not based on the fabulous profits made by merchants of rare ability but on the average earnings of the citizens in the village. According to the Government Industrial Survey of the Central Provinces & Berar the average income of a villager is about a rupee per month. From the taxes drawn from such persons it will be iniquitous to pay thousands a month to those who are supposed to serve them. The best of village industries cannot pay more than about Rs. 75/- per month per family. Hence, even a salary of Rs. 200/- per month for a Commissioner for a Division would be on the liberal side. That being so, all other emoluments will be scaled down accordingly. The fees of lawyers, doctors, etc. and the remuneration of engineers, teachers and other public servants will also fall in line. At present the princely salaries of Government servants are setting a standard completely out of keeping with the country's capacity to pay. It is this anomalous standard that is responsible for driving all the educated into clerical jobs. If we would have the educated to take interest in the villages, we have to alter this glamorous attraction to the desk. The Government being the largest single employer and spender, it has the responsibility of directing employment to desired channels by its planned expenditures. Our National Government has to take this into account. The Congress Government made a good beginning by limiting the highest salaries to Rs. 500/-. The full implication of this step is not often realised. It has far-reaching consequences.

Functions :

Apart from efficient administration, the Government has to play the important role of the chief partner in the business of the people. The economic activities of the nation can be controlled for better or for worse by the organization of Forests, Minerals, Power Resources and Communications.

Forests :

The forests represent the perennial reservoir from which the people will draw their raw materials for their industries. Our country is rich in forest wealth but it is not planned so as to supply the materials as and when the people need them. When a carpenter needs wood, he buys what he can in the market. Such wood is not seasoned; so the article he makes cracks or warps. Seasoning wood takes time and no carpenter can afford the capital to stock logs long enough to season nor would he have the space. It, therefore, falls to the lot of the Forest Department to season the wood in the forests before unloading it on the market. Similarly, there are thousand and one articles from the forest which can be controlled and regulated to supply the needs of the people and keep up the level of their economic activity. This aspect of the forest management is more or less ignored today. That which weighs with the Government is the revenue yielding capacity of forests.

Minerals :

Mines and quarries are the treasure trove of the people. Unlike the forests, these are likely to be exhausted by exploitation. Hence great care must be taken to make the best use of them. They represent potential employment for the people. When ores are sent out of the country, the heritage of the people of the land is being sold out. It is the birthright of the people to work on the ores and produce finished articles. Today, in India, most of the ores are being exported. We are, therefore, not only losing the opportunities of employment for the people but impoverishing the land. Minerals like other raw materials, have to be worked into consumable articles and only after that can the commerce part of the transaction commence. Any Government that countenances a foreign trade in the raw materials of a country is doing a disservice to the land. A Swaraj Government will not only organize the exploitation of the raw materials for the people but will help them to use these in their industries. Here is the rightful place for large scale industries under the control of the Government. A steel plant may produce steel bars and plates but not bolts and nuts. The latter should be the preserve of the village blacksmith.

Power :

Supply of cheap power and light can be undertaken by Government by harnessing the water power in the land. This, too, has to be directly under Government control.

Communications :

Roads, canals, railways, shipping and the like have to be provided by the Government. Apart from the paucity of canals, the railways have had a monopoly of transport for long distances. The flow of goods has been controlled by carefully scheduled discriminating special rates. This must be done in the interests of the people. Today through the instrumentality of these rates, such railways as we have have helped to drain raw materials from the land, and to bring foreign manufactures into the remotest villages. This policy has been one that has brought the ruin of industry in India in no small measure. To give only one instance, in connection with the oil-pressing industry which is one of the large industries of India, if one takes 100 maunds of Mahua seeds to Bombay from C. P., it costs Rs. 46-6-0, but if the oil is pressed at Akola, C. P., and the oil and cake from 100 maunds Mahua seeds are transported to Bombay, it costs Rs. 77-15-0. This means that the oil press in C. P. has a handicap of Rs. 31-9-0 per 100 maunds on the freight alone, and that the tendency of the seed, therefore, is to go to Bombay. There are over ten thousand such special rates. A National Government will undo this injustice at the first possible moment, and control the traffic in the interests of the villagers' economic activity. The railway may be a good instrument but can be used effectively to impoverish the people by depriving them of employment.

Taxation :

To carry out their work the Government has to find the wherewithal. This comes from taxation. We have to be careful to see that the incidence of taxation does not fall unduly heavily on the taxpayer who is below the subsistence level. When the taxes are collected, the expenditures of Government should be so made as to increase the taxable capacity of the citizen. When the taxes are gathered from the villagers, and the expenses which benefit the towns are met out of them, impoverishment of the people results. We have already seen one safeguard in the scale of salaries: another important safety valve is in the collection of taxes in kind. However inconvenient it may be to gather taxes in kind, such an exchange prevents marginal loss in the national income. The allowances to officials can be met partly in kind. This old system still prevails in most of the Muslim countries. In the Pathan states of the N. W. F. P., it is working well to this day.

Expenditure :

When taxes are received from one area and much of them are spent in another, impoverishment of the former takes place. If money received from the farmers is spent on buildings in New Delhi, the country is the poorer for it. As far as possible tax moneys must be spent as near the place of collection as possible. Cheapness of a foreign article may be a consideration for a private citizen but not to the Government. If the Government spends tax money for paper from Sweden, it is against the interests of the taxpayer if paper made locally can be obtained. If the Government pays one anna for foreign paper and the local paper can be had for one and a half annas, even this higher price is more economical from the country's point of view. In the first case one anna goes out of the country; a local purchase, on the other hand, gives employment to the taxpayer and keeps the money in circulation. Hence, all Government expenditures must, as far as possible, be spent within the "catchment" area of taxation.

Large Scale Industries :

Large scale industries control the life of several individuals. In a true democracy no private citizen should have this power. Therefore, all large scale industries must be State-owned and State-managed. Most such industries cannot run without various forms of help from the Government. We have already mentioned discriminations in freight rates. For large scale productions various conveniences, such as ports, quays, docks and railways are needed. When these are provided at the expense of the taxpayer's money, such benefits, if extended to private concerns, become subsidies out of public monies to concerns run for private profit. This cannot be allowed. Tax money must be spent for the general benefit. From this point of view also all such large scale industries must be run by the State.

Large scale industries are needed in exploiting natural resources which should form the raw materials of the peoples' industries. Control of such raw materials cannot be left in private hands. Therefore, all such industries should also be under the State. Large scale industry in economics is the antithesis of democracy in politics. It is not by chance that the Western nations have come by their economic organization. It is a result of their way of thinking in terms of autocracy. They find themselves with dictatorships in political organization and centralized industries in the economic field. These two go together and we cannot have the one without the other.

If we aim at true democracy, we have to abandon centralized production in consumption goods. This does not preclude all centralized industries. As we have already seen, there is a definite field for such, though restricted. Within these limits of Government controlled and owned industries supplying raw materials to the people, providing public utilities and manufacturing instruments etc., there is a large field of work for such units. Just as certain chemicals used in minute quantities may prove to be healing potions and when used in large doses may prove fatal poisons, so also cantralized units can be a blessing to the people when properly co-ordinated with the peoples' economic activities and not used for the exploitation of the masses. This can only be done when such industries are run on a service basis even at a loss. Therefore, their natural place is only as a part of the Government organization of the country.

ECONOMIC ACTIVITY

People should have freedom to occupy themselves in supplying their own demands. How this can be planned is simple. Restricted profit motive is a good regulator of industries. The problem before the world today is not one of production but one of distribution. Hence, any method we decide on has to be a good distributor.

Distribution :

The wealth of a nation consists not in what a few possess but in the extent to which the majority can satisfy their daily wants, especially needs. Looked at from this angle, increase in the number of millionaries in a country need not indicate increase in the prosperity of the nation. Indeed, it may indicate the opposite if the accumulated wealth was occasioned by restricted distribution. When judging the well-being of nation, our consideration should centre round the way in which purchasing power is distributed among the citizens. If we adopt this criterion then industries which distribute wealth are better for the masses than industries that help a few to accumulate a great store of riches. This means that mills, which being centralized assist in accumulating wealth, are detrimental to the interests of the masses; and cottage industries, which distribute wealth are by far the better method to adopt, especially in our country where we are faced with a shortage not of labour but of capital. Therefore, the method of economic organization we choose must be one which takes this factor into consideration.

The centralized methods of production accumulate wealth and power in the hands of a few, and require considerable amount of accumulated capital to start with. This last factor removes such methods from within the reach of the masses, and does not fulfil our requirements as a distributor. Capitalistic systems and centralization are based on the presumption of capital being available. In our country, where such accumulated wealth is scarce and poverty is widespread, we have to found our organization on revenue. That means that the whole system must depend for its efficient working on the day-to-day labour of the people. A palace built with high skilled labour has to be repaired and kept in order by skilled labour but a hut built with mud can be kept clean by the inhabitants themselves with their own labour. The former presumes availability of capital but the latter is based on the availability of labour.

Planned Economy :

The welfare of a community depends on a well maintained balance of occupations, like health depends on a well balanced diet. In every village there should be a small number of artisans who supply the needs of the village. Man needs other things besides bread—the staple food. If all take to agriculture the community will suffer from a mal-distribution of its talents—a social deficiency disease. This is mainly the trouble in India. For instance, the old goldsmiths have lost their calling and their deft fingers have to break stones for road making. The accumulated skill of centuries of the Hindu artisan is now running to waste which is a loss to the progress of the human race itself. With the changing requirements of modern life the old time goldsmiths would have been well utilized in making such articles as are in great demand today, say watches, timepieces etc. India imports these and lets her skilled sons starve for lack of work.

Division of Labour :

The work a person is engaged in and the daily duties he performs must be such as to contribute to the fullest development of his personality. Sub-division of processes, which is necessary for standardized production under centralized methods, provides no scope for originality nor for the play of initiative. The worker in a centralized industry becomes a mere cogwheel of the huge machine. He loses his individuality and freedom of action.

The people of our land are extremely poor. Labour is plentiful but capital is scarce. A non-violent society must, therefore, be based on revenue and not on capital. These considerations lead us to advocate methods of production which involve little or no capital, and for which raw materials and a ready local market for finished products are easily available. However much we may desire it otherwise, we cannot change these factors, and any planning which ignores these will not succeed. Therefore, we are logically driven to the position which envisages village industries as the central occupation of the people. For these and other reasons we had cited under "Large Scale Industries" we cannot recommend the centralized methods of production for the masses.

Ahimsak Swadeshi :

Formerly, apart from speeches, the real economic drive began with the Swadeshi Movement, following the partition of Bengal. At that time the idea of Swadeshi was purely political *i.e.*, Indian made articles as against foreign made goods. Gandhiji was quick to discern that the downfall of India was due more to economic causes than political ones, and he bravely shouldered single-handed, the burden, ridicule and ignominy of the Charkha Movement. This watered the seeds of life in villages and bound him with hoops of steel to the heart of the masses. When as a consequence of the Charkha Movement, boycott of foreign cloth began, people became accustomed to self-denying ordinances which were stronger and more formidable than any tariff that can be imposed by the might of Great Britain. The Big Bertha of non-violence knocked the base out of Manchester more effectively than any long-range gun yet conceived by man.

Political Swadeshi may mean goods produced within certain political or geographical boundaries. In this there may be no need for moral values and it may lead to hatred when foreign goods are boycotted from such considerations. Refraining from buying goods which are not manufactured by one's neighbours carries no such hatred but is a sign of one's own limitations. The political boycott may lead to war but true Swadeshi will knit neighbours together. True Swadeshi seeks to discharge the responsibilities of a consumer or buyer as a trustee. A business transaction does not begin and end with the transfer of goods and payment of money ; in addition, it involves the consideration of one's duties to one's fellow men.

Centralization is nothing and decentralization is nothing if we have not the love that binds man and man. We are often told that Japan uses the cottage method largely. We have to see if the final effect is for the good of all people. If Japan uses the cottage method to exploit China, we can no more tolerate that than centralized industries. Recently Gandhiji issued a warning to the public not to buy Khadi from uncertified dealers. What is the difference ? Materially there is no difference, but viewed from the moral and humane standpoint there is a world of difference. The A.I.S.A. insists on a subsistence wage being paid to the producers, therefore the Charkha Sangh Khadi is honest cloth, bearing its cost; while the other may be the result of exploitation and hence may be said to include human misery in its composition. Hence, we must beware of even decentralized industries. One who would want to be sure of the moral purity of an article should buy articles manufactured under his range of knowledge. This is the Gandhian interpretation of Swadeshi.

Costs :

A great part of the money spent on cottage-made articles goes towards payment of wages. The materials themselves cost very little, but in mill-made articles while the least expense is on labour the bulk is for overhead charges, sales organization and materials. Economics of the manufacturers of the West are dictated by low prices, but for the prosperity of an agricultural people high prices are welcome. High prices of cottage industry products also help in the distribution of wealth which means they contribute largely to the welfare of the people.

Self-help :

The capitalistic system depends for its development on the helplessness of its customers. The more helpless the customer the more sure it is of its markets. It seeks to kill all initiative in the customer. Indeed, the capitalistic structure is raised on the foundation of tombstones of the initiative of the customers. In cottage industries the principal desideratum is the consumer's initiative; we expect every one to be resourceful.

Exhibitions :

Under capitalism, exhibitions are organized to attract sales, *i.e.*, to increase the demand after the supply comes into existence. This is putting the cart before the horse. The Gandhian scheme would transform exhibitions into a form of adult education by placing before the public the various stages of production during which raw materials get transformed into finished goods. Such exhibitions should also demonstrate improvements made in processes and instruments. Ultimately, such temporary exhibitions should become permanent Sangrahalayas. Capitalist producers carry on their own experiments and keep the results as their own secrets, but we have to strive to disseminate such knowledge as we possess to the producers by means of exhibitions.

Business transactions do not begin and end with the transfer of goods and payment of money. One who buys an article takes it with all the moral values attached to the goods. If one buys a stolen article one becomes party to that offence. This is the responsibility and trusteeship of wealth. So it is the duty of every consumer to know the conditions under which things he needs are produced. If he patronises goods made under objectionable conditions he becomes a party to it. Hence, it is necessary to organize such exhibitions also from the point of view of the consumer. When properly arranged, they should also educate the public to realise the duties of a purchaser and consumer, and enable the latter to fulfil his duties by placing before him the chances of getting goods he needs produced under conditions which would meet with his approval.

CHAPTER 16 INDUSTRIAL PROGRAMME

It is impossible to overlook in any country the organization needed to provide food and other primary necessities. Agriculture ought, therefore, to be the greatest amongst occupations. To carry on this occupation profitably, we require a considerable and close study of nature on a scientific basis, for it is an occupation in which man attempts to control nature and his own environment in such a way as to produce the best results. This work cannot possibly be carried on individualistically, because it requires a considerable amount of time for experimentation, going often beyond the proverbial three score years and ten which may fall to the lot of the long lived ones. Many of the experiments in-cross-breeding to bring out special strains in particular crops have to be tested through several generations before they can be put into the practical field on a commercial scale. This type of work can only be done by the State for the people, and when it is done, unless the result of the experimentation is brought home to the cultivator and he is afforded every encouragement to carry it on, it will be useless. Merely improving tools without considering the conditions under which the man works, will not solve the problem.

Next to agriculture, probably, the greatest industry is the production of clothing. This may be used as a subsidiary industry to agriculture which, in our country, hardly occupies even half the working days in a year. If we can usefully employ the idle hours of the farmer, that in itself will afford sufficient wealth to increase greatly the purchasing power of the people. This is a line in which a wise attempt has been made and considerable success achieved by the programme of work laid out by the All-India Spinner's Association.

There are also other industries which help to decrease the pressure on land by drawing off the idle population and providing work for them. We may divide these into (a) industries which affect the whole country because the products are in universal demand, and (b) cottage industries which provide curious and luxury articles.

Though in a general way people have an idea of the type of industries we inclue under the category of Village, Cottage and Home Industries, yet at the present time, as the Governments are introducing these terms into their administrative directions etc., it would be well to have a clear conception of the feature by which we may identify and classify them uniformly.

I. Industries which answer all or most of the following conditions may be considered *Village Industries* :

(i) Those that manufacture indispensable articles needed in villages and for villagers.

(ii) Using processes within the easy reach of villagers

(iii) With the help of tools and implements falling within the financial capacity of the villagers carrying on the industry.

(iv) Utilizing local raw materials.

(v) With the aid of human or animal power.

(vi) Meeting the demand of local or nearby markets.

(vii) Not causing displacement of labour or unemployment among wage earners.

Some of these industries may need the co-operation of many workers which may be secured by sharing profit or by payment of daily wages. The number of wage earners in a unit may differ from industry to industry.

Examples :

Oil Pressing, Weaving, Tanning, Carpentry, Blacksmithy etc.

II. *Cottage Industries* are whole time occupations that do not require factory buildings with elaborate or special plant and equipment but can be engaged in by the workers in their own cottages.

Examples :

Gold & Silver Smithy, Shoe-making, Tailoring etc.

III. *Home Industries* are those carried on practically, by the members of the family, in their spare time.

Examples :

Spinning, Fruit Preserving, Needlework, Bee-keeping, Embroidery etc.

Financing of any of the above units or types of industries may be undertaken by the units themselves or raised by co-operation among those engaged in the industry.

Village Industries :

Under the first group we may bring in occupations which are closely connected with the production of food from raw materials, such as flour-grinding, dehusking of paddy, oil-pressing, gur-making etc. Then there are other industries which may provide universal subsidiary occupations to the agriculturists such as bee-keeping, sericulture, lac-cultivation etc.

Then we have many occupations which touch definite communities but, at the same time, are spread over the whole country, such as tanning, paper-making, rope-making basket-making, pottery, bricks, tiles, carpentry, blacksmithy etc. These industries may well be called the main village industries.

Cottage Industries :

Apart from these, under the second group, we have cottage industries for the manufacture of luxury articles and others, the demand for which may not be so universal but which are in use every day, such as soap-making, printing, dyeing, works of art, metal industries etc. Unless we have our industries broad-based and well organized to supplement each other, the country cannot be an economic unit.

As we have already seen, international trade should only be confined to such articles as cannot be consumed locally, because, owing to the present economic barriers to be met with even within our own country, it is not possible to ensure full returns to the producer. As long as this state of affairs continues, and the producer has no hold on international markets and is not well enough equipped to understand their working, it will be suicidal for him to attempt to go beyond the borders of our land. As far as practicable, we have to attempt to convert raw materials into finished products before they leave the locality in which the raw materials are found.

When raw materials are exported it is equivalent to exporting employment. Therefore the import of finished goods which can be made from raw materials available locally, is creating unemployment. This immediately gives us the solution to this problem. The more we use locally made goods the less will the unemployed be.

A. I. V. I. A. Programme :

The All India Village Industries Association has been formed to carry out this function. The method adopted by this Association may be divided into three groups :

(1) It tries to stop wastage and to convert waste materials to good purpose.

(2) It attempts to conserve the resources at present available to the villagers.

(3) It attempts to utilize profitably the hours of leisure and introduce such work as will increase the wealth of the people.

As an instance of the first item on the programme, we may mention the question of nutrition, sanitation and hygiene. Situated as we are, man is the most important factor and motive power in our economic system. If he is allowed to remain in an under-nourished condition and is weakened by various diseases, then production suffers. A balanced diet therefore, becomes a necessity. As it is, many of our villagers have barely sufficient cereal to consume. They have practically no vegetables or other elements that are necessary to supply the requirements of the body. It is, therefore, a criminal waste for them to consume whatever cereal is available to them in a nutritively depleted form, as they now do. This is what happens, for example, when they get their rice polished in a mill, depriving the grains of the bran, mineral salts, oils and pericarp, and leaving mainly the starch for food. It is not possible to go into all the details of the programme of the Association here, but this is stated merely as an illustration to indicate the method of which the problem is attacked.

In regard to the effort to conserve the resources at present available, we may mention the attempt to utilize night soil and village waste in the form of manure, as well as the programme for the disposal of carcasses whereby every part of the dead animals is used.

To illustrate the effort made to increase productivity, we may mention the attempt to introduce subsidiary occupations such as bee-keeping, paper-making, lac-culture etc.

What to Produce :

The main purpose is to make production as broad based as possible and to aim at producing goods which the people themselves require rather than attempt the production of articles required by the wealthy. As long as we produce articles which are in universal demand, such as simple cotton clothing, village chappals, sleeping mats etc., the problem of marketing does not arise. When production aims at supplying the needs of the wealthy, though the margin of profit may be higher, yet the difficulties of marketing shift the gains of the occupation to the middleman. Also the number of people who can be profitably occupied becomes very small as the demand for such goods is confined to the rich.

Our purpose should be to distribute wealth amongst as many persons as possible and not to concentrate it in a few hands. Where articles required a little help in their marketing the Association attempted to do this also by introducing the producer and the consumer to each other through the medium of certified shops located in towns and cities, but the main emphasis is not on such goods as require this help.

The Association keeps in mind the poverty of the masses and advocates only such industries as require little or no capital, need simple equipment, are easy in technique and the manufactures of which find a ready market. The raw material should be locally available, but if it is imported then the cost of such raw material should bear a very low percentage to the total cost of the finished product. If brass sheets are imported from abroad, and the beaten brass vessel sells at Rs. 4/- of which Rs. 3/- represents the cost of the brass sheet, then obviously 75% of the price paid finds its ways out into distant markets. The remedy is to find substitutes for such vessels and stop our purchasing power being transferred to distant places. Production should be centred round the needs of the villagers, and under present conditions, international trade should be at a discount. Things that provide the villagers with better food, clothes and shelter should be emphasised rather than articles meant for distant markets. Some missionaries have been attempting to introduce poultry keeping in village, but their methods are not suitable. They introduce foreign birds such as Leghorns, Minorcas, Rhode Island Reds, and their cross-breeds. The eggs show a great improvement in size and the birds are fine, but the villager cannot afford to eat such eggs himself and so he sells them to city-folk. The birds themselves are very expensive, need careful looking after and are not as resistance to disease as country fowl. If an epidemic comes, the whole stock often dies. Such industry is speculative and therefore, beyond the capacity of our villagers. We would prefer to see an improvement in the eggs of the country fowl and feel satisfied if the villagers themselves eat the eggs and sell only the surplus. Catering to a distant market makes them depend on the tender mercies of middlemen.

It is often argued that anything that puts money into the villagers' pockets is good. This is a partial truth. Money economy is essential to extend the market. Distant suppliers demand money, therefore, putting more money into the pockets of the villagers is increasing the chances of sale of foreign products and reducing employment in our own land. We know to our cost the truth of this statement. Who will advocate the villager selling his milk for money and starving his own child ?

When we import foreign articles, we forget that we are throwing the bread of our children away to others and thus increasing the unemployed and partly employed. We are in effect, using foreign servants. We are too poor to be able to do this. We cannot go on consuming without producing. We should try to see that all locally available raw materials are turned into finished articles before being marketed.

At present, all our industries are slowly becoming curio trades. Every trade, the articles of which are widely used in our households gives employment to several persons and the articles themselves are low priced. But the moment a trade shifts to cater for the curio hunter, the article manufactured is a diminutive replica of the original and finds no market as a household article although it may fetch a higher price. The number of workers engaged in the trade accordingly diminishes and middlemen appear to exploit the profits. Hence, such curio trades are not really in the national interests.

As the programme stands, women can play an unrivalled part in building our frame-work on a solid foundation. Practically the whole of the programme lies within the sphere of women—sanitation, hygiene, nutrition, clothing, and household requirements. If women will make up their minds that they will not buy goods which have been produced by exploitation and go in only for articles produced in decentralized way, they will give a great impetus to the revival of our countryside and place the nation on a sound economic basis.

The Association also attempts to provide expert technical advice and help to improve our age-old methods of production.

By such efforts, if we can safeguard the masses from the exploiters, if we can give them employment to fill their idle moments, if we can direct their activity into industries which have a ready and known demand, if we can help to increase their productivity without resorting to predation, if locally available raw materials can be worked up in the most scientific way, then the nation will surely emerge from the slough of despond to a rock of hope and thence march on to prosperity.

CHAPTER 17 CENTRALIZATION vs. DECENTRALIZATION

In this chapter we shall gather together all the arguments, for and against the two forms of organizing production of goods for consumption even at the risk of some repetition.

Every instrument has to be shaped to fulfil the purpose for which it is intended if it is to function efficiently. We cannot drive a nail into the wall with a watch nor cut a furrow through the field with a penknife. We should use a hammer for the first and plough for the second, for the purpose. If this is so in the mechanical world, how much more important it is to use proper methods in the Social and Economic Spheres.

Yet how many give any thought to fitness of instruments they recommended as the means ? Centralization or decentralization methods are but instruments for social and economic ends. Therefore, we have to weigh carefully the claims of either systems to suit our purpose, before we can launch out on a definite programme.

The Goal of an Economic System :

No one of us is likely to question the purpose of an economic order which may be stated for clarity's sake as follows :

(1) It should create wealth as efficiently as possible.
(2) It should distribute wealth widely and evenly.
(3) It should supply the needs of the people before comforts and luxuries are catered for.

(4) It should be a means for eliciting all the faculties of the worker and developing his personality.

(5) It should be conducive to peace and harmony of society.

Circumstances leading to Centralization :

Centralization has been the result of five main causes—

(1) Where there is to be found accumulated capital with a few persons who seek to keep a close and watchful eye over their investment, they prefer centralized methods. We find a good example of this in Great Britain. When she got the hoarded wealth of India, she resorted to this form of production in the eighteenth century.

(2) When there is a good deal of pressing work and there is a scarcity of labour, perforce man grows extra hands in the form of tools or mechanism. A good example of this the growth of industrialization in U.S.A. America's vast distances, virgin forests and mighty rivers obstructed man's progress through the continent. People who could be harnessed to this work were few, hence the great conquest of natural forces

(3) Wherever standardised articles are needed, centralization is essential to multiply a particular kind of article on a mass scale. Such need may arise out of two causes : (*a*) Functionally, where the article by its very nature calls for standard parts, *e.g.*, motor cars, railway rolling stock etc., and (*b*) purposive, where it is necessary because large numbers need identically similar articles as in the case of military equipment; examples of this may be seen in the

militaristic nations of today, Italy, Germany and Japan.

(4) Centralization in production may again be resorted to where labour is plentiful and it has to be manoeuvered to a plan of work as in the case of Soviet Russia where regimentation of labour was resorted to bring about quick results.

(5) Again it may be necessary when raw materials, manufactures and markets are wide apart. It is only by unified control that these can be brought together so as to enable the machines to produce steadily and at an economic speed. Japan, Germany and England furnish good examples of these.

Evils of Centralization :

We have mentioned only five, but these are not inseparable. In some countries more than one factor may bring about centralized production. These situations considered above are to a great extent solved by resorting to centralized production but the evils attaching to such a method are not avoided. These evils again may be seen to correspond to the five causes :

(1) Centralization, which is the result of accumulation of capital, also leads to concentration of wealth which is the hot-bed of class cleavages.

(2) When scarcity of labour drives men to methods of centralized production, naturally the labour force being few, purchasing power distributed in the process of production is also small. Therefore this inevitably leads to shortage in purchasing power and ultimately decreases the effectiveness of the demand and thus causes relative overproduction, such as the one we witness in the world today.

(3) Where need for standardization brings about centralization of production, there can be no variegation in the product. It also checks progress. By facilitating large scale equipment, it encourages warfare.

(4) Regimentation of labour leads to a greater concentration of power which is even more dangerous than concentration of wealth. The greater the numbers held by central control the greater can the power be.

(5) Co-ordination of supplies of raw materials, production and finding markets for finished goods results in imperialism and warfare.

Decentralization

Let us now turn towards decentralization and consider under which circumstances it can be used with advantage. Here again we shall look at the problem from the corresponding five points :

(1) Where there is a scarcity of capital, it is not possible nor is it necessary to have centralization. The only possibility is decentralization. An attempt is being made to meet this by the promotion of Limited Liability Companies to gather in scattered bits of capital but this does not solve the problem of distribution of wealth. It presents other difficulties.

(2) Where there is a plethora of labour, or in other words, unemployment or under-employment, we shall be increasing the malady by centralizing the production.

(3) Diversity and variegation is the very essence of decentralization. Where this is needed no machine

can compete with hand-work, more especially where the hand-work has to be the expression of a personality.

(4) If democracy is to be attained, decentralization lays the required foundation. As centralization kills all initiative in the masses, they succumb readily to central dictatorship. Centralization is the grave of democracy.

(5) Where raw materials and markets are in the proximity of the producing centres, decentralization methods will serve well.

Advantages :

(1) Decentralization makes for more even distribution of wealth and makes people tolerant.

(2) The process of production includes distribution of wealth also, as a large part of the cost goes to pay for the labour. Better distribution of purchasing power leads to effective demand and production is directed into a supply of needs as the supply here will follow demand.

(3) As each producer becomes an entrepreneur, he gets plenty of scope to exercise his initiative. With the responsibility of the business on his shoulders, business-like methods and habits will be formed. When every individual develops himself, the average intelligence of the nation will increase.

(4) The market being close to the centre of production, there is not much difficulty in selling the goods nor have we to create an artificial market by forced salesmanship.

(5) Without centralization of either wealth or power there can be no disturbance of peace on a large nationwide scale.

A glance at the above analysis should leave no doubt as to what will suit conditions in our own country. Of course as regards key industries and public utilities there is no alternative to centralization, but this can be done either co-operatively or by socialising such industries.

It must be clearly remembered that when we advocate decentralization, it does not mean that we eschew all machinery. Where machines work as tools or slaves of man we need them and have to improve the existing ones. It is only when machine is used to transfer the benefit of one man's labour to another that we have to cry a halt.

Under such circumstances, machine becomes the master and man becomes a slave. As far as circumstances in our country go, decentralized methods are the only remedy for the ills we suffer from—lack of initiative, want of sense of responsibility, looseness in business methods, wide-spread poverty, un-employment and under-employment.

Decentralized methods of production have an educative value which no nation that wishes to progress and is willing to take advantage of every opportunity open to it for the purpose, can afford to ignore with impunity. Centralized methods of production offer no such educational values to the worker : on the contrary its strain and stress makes the man deteriorate whatever material contributions it may make to his animal needs. Let us not therefore blindly follow the shadow and lose the substance.

CHAPTER 18 EDUCATION FOR LIFE

In the last analysis we are led to the conclusion that all problems radiate from education. We can solve our difficulties only by educating the people to view life from a common standpoint. Education is a master key that gives admission into all departments that make up life.

Meaning of Education :

What do we mean by education ? Is it a certain type of schooling that begins after a child reaches the age of five and finishes, according to the means the parents possess, when the child reaches youth ? Is it merely literary, or occupational or utilitarion ? Is it an end or a means ? Has it a beginning ? Has it a finishing ? What we have to consider will depend upon the conception we have of education.

If education is to fit us for life—to make us better citizens, better husbands and better fathers—it has to be a continuous process from the cradle to the grave. Through all the changing scenes of life we ought to be able to pass with the least shock. If, on the other hand, education taught us only certain tricks which we could perform, we should be completely at sea when a different set of circumstances confronted us. Education need not cramp our minds with facts and figures but it should give us an attitude towards life.

An educational system has to have a philosophy behind it and its purpose should be to elicit the best in an individual. Therefore, the undertaking of education is a grave responsibility fraught with many dangers and we cannot launch out lightly upon any scheme without proper preparation and thought.

Unfortunately, the system of spreading the art of reading and writing has been often identified with education. Nothing can be more grotesque. Reading and writing are means of acquiring culture but they are not the only means nor are they the most important means.

Education with a Purpose :

In most countries, at present, education has a definite purpose or goal. In capitalistic countries, the captains of industry look upon it as a nursery for their future executive and administrators. In socialist countries, they harness it to increase material production. In militaristic nations, education means a creation of a narrow patriotism.

In the First Stage of Imperialism

In a bureaucracy, like the one we have in our country, it has been the provider of clerks. It was with this end that Macaulay enunciated the first principles of his educational system for our country. On these principles all our universities have been built since then. With what success this system has worked its havoc we all know to our sorrow. We need only look around to see the clerical mind in high places—Professors, Administrators, Lawyers, Judges and even acting Governors of provinces are drawn from mental training that befits clerks—those who are there are there to obey and carry out orders. Initiative and original thinking are decided disadvantages in a clerk. Today our country is filled with men with the clerical mind in all walks of life. There is considerable truth in the statement that we are not fit to govern ourselves. Directly in proportion too the measure in which we had taken advantage of the education provided in our universities have we become unfit to govern ourselves. The university has been the means of creating in the best of us what is come to be known as an inferiority complex and diffidence in ourselves. Clerks cannot govern themselves, they depend on the orders of others. Tilaks and Gandhis have broken away from the trappings as they were naturally too great for the mental cage of clerks. The production of English knowing clerks for the working of a well-organized and disciplined system of Government was a primary requirement in the first stage of British Imperialism.

In the Second Stage of Imperialism :

The second stage of imperialism has now come, with a settled Government, the better exploitation of natural resources is the next step. For this clerk-minded men are useless. While a few may be absorbed in the offices they will find themselves out of their elements in workshops and factories as their physical faculties have been paralysed. It is not practicable to get such men out from Great Britain. It is better to train such foremen, fitters and machine-men locally. The literary education given so far is no good. The system has got to be changed. Before doing so an enquiry by expert educationists had to be conducted. This is the work that had been done by Messrs Abbott and Wood.

In their published report (Report on *Vocational Education in India*, by A. Abbott and S. H. Wood) they hold that general education is the earlier and vocational education the later phase of a full system of education. In fact, they look upon vocational education as the extension of general education. In this they are diametrically opposed to Gandhiji's views. They advocate that vocational education should be given in full regard to the development of organized industry, industrialization of the country and prosperity will then follow. They acknowledge the futility of the present type of education to develop character. They claim vocational training ought to make the pupil diligent, accurate, self-reliant and resourceful and teach him to co-operate with others. Their anxiety is not to cater for the managerial posts which can take care of themselves, but to provide for the supervisory grades and the operative sections. They say "the foreman holds in fact the key to efficiency in production". Again they state, "The pressing need of organized industry in India is not for any considerable addition to the supply of highly trained men looking for managerial posts after having had some experience of industry, but for better trained foremen". (P. 63) Their whole view point is focussed on the better exploitation of the resources of the country and not on the training of the individual. They are also only considering the facilities to be given to the big man's business. "While we firmly believe that it is right to begin the systematic expansion of the facilities for training the workers of various grades on whom the effective conduct of organized industry depends, we hope, that this expansion will not be so swift as to overtake that of organized industry itself". (P. 42) Their interest in the welfare of masses is nowhere visible. The vocational training begins and ends with the needs of big industry. Such education, as this report suggests, should be no concern of the Government. The organized industries should be quite capable of looking after themselves and training such men as are needed for their working. One would expect a committee, on which public money is being spent, would be required to suggest ways and means of improving the educational training of the largest number of workers. But the interest of the rural population is dismissed with the following quotation from the Royal Commission on Agriculture (1928) with which opinion their entire agreement is expressed. "The chief solution of the problems of the cultivator is the intensification or diversification of his agriculture"and that "the possibilities of improving the conditions of the rural population by the establishment of rural industries are extremely limited".

So this report appears to be a natural corollary to Macaulay's minute and follows logically from it.

The Oriental Method :

In our own country, the system of education followed in the past was a training ground for life. A student chose his master and lived his everyday life under his master's watchful eye and imbibed the spirit of his *guru*. This was the case, not merely with spiritual training, but in every walk of life. The *guru* himself did not look upon teaching as a profession any more than a father looks upon his parental duties as a profession. The *guru* led his own life from which emanated his outlook on life and his disciple gleaned what he could from his practice. Jesus, when he chose his disciples, said "follow me" and he did not give them a list of text books to read. They had to follow in their master's footsteps. That is our system of education.

The Occidental Way :

According to Western ideas education is looked upon as a profession which is a glorified name for a trade. In India, it had become a retail trade. The so-called professors and teachers are there making a living just as a petty shop-keeper gathers in his profits. The petty shop-keeper buys his goods from the wholesale and sells it to the consumer. Similarly the Indian Professor of Economics gets his goods from Marshal,

Pigou or Government reports and retails it to his students. Hence, there need be no more love for the subject than the shop-keeper has for the commodity he sells or for the buyer. The profit or the salary is the power that attracts the professors or teachers. If we make the remuneration just sufficient to meet the necessities of life how many will care for their jobs ? In the old system each village had lands set apart for its schools and thus the needs of the teacher were provided for. Today, the mercenary educationist needs as large a profit out of his business as a well-to-do merchant in a large city to attract him to the job. This is altogether contrary to the ideals of true education as was found in our land.

History of Educational Reform :

Reformers have recognized the anomaly but have not yet found a way out of it. When the Civil Disobedience Movement called out students from colleges and schools it revealed how futile the leaders considered was the education that was imparted. Though we had nothing to replace the then existing system, yet it was felt that the so-called education given in the universities was worse than no education at all. Remaining away from schools and colleges was in itself a gain as we were abstraining from putting our youth through the clerical mould provided for use by the alien Government.

After this first step, attempts were made to give some kind of education. The various Vidhyapiths sprang up. The main difference between the universities and these innovations lay in the choice of the media for imparting knowledge. Where English had the predominance now the provincial language came into its own. Apart from this the syllabus was little altered. Educationists were thinking hard as to the type that would be best suited to serve the needs of the nation. This resulted a few years later in introducing manual labour in the form of an industry or a handicraft. Gradually about half the time was spent in such labour and half in so called cultural subjects. This went on till a couple of years ago. This method of education produced men with more character but they could not be termed ideal villagers. These institutions were mostly in large towns and young men were being weaned from village life. The attractions of town life to an undeveloped youth were too strong to resist. The students after passing out of the Vidyapiths thought in terms of the country's needs but beyond propaganda and some organizing they were not able to carry out much constructive work. They could only be birds of passage in villages. However much their influence counted for good, it was not permanent.

When the A. I. V. I. A. was started a need was felt for trained village workers. The methods of Vidyapith were tried in vain. The need was to find men who would settle down in the midst of villagers and shed their light around them so that they might be a source of inspiration and comfort to those whose lot is cast in rural areas. It was useless sending men with an inclination towards city life into villages. We needed true types of villagers trained to lead others by their example. It was imperative that our students be ideal villagers leading the ordinary life of villagers. They should support themselves just as any other villager does by his own effort with the help of an industry. To this end our school was remodelled to give the student an opportunity to learn at least one industry by which he can support himself. This learning of one industry is the central feature but around this he has to be taught all other subjects. This in a greater measure contains the old principle of fitting a person for life. It is not yet time to examine the results of this experiment. Every person influences for good or bad those around him. If we can so arrange that we are able to spread good influence by placing trained men in villages, the problem will be solved to a great extent.

True Values :

1. FINANCIAL

Unfortunately, the present products of our universities have apishly followed the standards of living set before us by foreigners. These people are looked upto—rightly or wrongly—by villagers with disastrous results. False standards of value have been gaining ground in the remotest of villages. The villager has been attempting to live beyond his means in an effort to imitate the example of towns-folk. This has made him sink further into the quick-sand of debt. His desire for imported finery is taking away all available forms of employment. The more foreign articles are bought the greater becomes our own unemployment and the deeper our poverty. Our education has to touch all walks of life in a village. We have to show by demonstration how a villager's life should be ordered. Standards of value have to be evolved and inculcated. They should be such as will lead to the welfare of the villagers.

2. SOCIAL

Our methods have become so far removed from the right path that our very life kills us. In trying to imitate the shadow we lose the substance. Not long ago I visited a seat of Sanskrit learning. I was pained to see how far they had drifted away from real culture. They would teach certain *mantras* to a particular sect of *Brahmins*. It is needless to say no *Harijans* were allowed in the College. Is this culture? Where are the true *Brahmins* in India, when we get our "education" from the 'British ? Where are the *Kshatriyas* when we are under foreign domination ? Where are the *Vaishyas* when the country is groaning under British exploitation ? If there be a *Brahmin*, if there be a *Kshatriya*, if there be a *Vaishya* it is only the Britisher. Is it not pathetic that in our degradation some of us, untouchables of the world, should pretend we are Brahmins and instead of carrying the torch of enlightenment to the remotest corners,attempt to hide our light under a bushel ? Can there be anything more heart-rending than the pride and arrogance of these untouchable Brahmins of our land ? Learning ancient lore is no more culture than vomitting is digesting. As a cow eats grass and yields milk so also if we learn ancient lore and by contact with present-day problems are able to convert that knowledge to practice and transform the evils of present society into good, then only can we call it true culture. There can be no culture without contact with relevant problems. Much learning is possible to have in a library but no culture. That institution was making walking volumes of men but it cannot impart culture as long as it keeps itself aloof from the world. Such institutions are parasitic and should be wiped out of existence. These are disease germs breeding centres of our educational system. True education is above all castes and creeds. It transcends man-made bounds. Until we recognize the dignity of all human beings we shall be bound by so called "sacred threads" to death's -head and degradation. Let us shake ourselves loose from such bondage. If there be any who feels proud that he is a *Brahmin* may he know that India has to bow down her head in shame before the world because of such unnatural distinctions.

The *Brahmin*, who was originally intended to be the custodian of the purity of the race and the trustee of national culture, has misappropriated these privileges and has contrived by various means to keep himself segregated from his fellow-beings. By these means the *Brahmins* are rapidly losing their former position of responsibility and leadership. It is very like the case of a medical man, who in order to avoid contagion or infection from sick people, abandons his profession and confines himself in a germproof cell. Such a person, instead of protecting society from danger, is a prasite himself.

This idea of utouchability and the grades of respectability in caste are things which have to be jettisoned before the Goddess culture will deign to look at us.

3. ECONOMIC

The close contact of Western commerce has enshrined gold amongst us. Our cultural values have yield place to money values. We have begun to think in terms of gold and not in terms of humanity. The Brahminical cultural standards have gone and the Baniya civilization of the West has crept in. The *Brahmin* was valued and respected not because of his possession but because of the service he was to render to society without regard to the return he gets. No educational system, which does not place first things first, is worthy of our attention. Any attempt to educate the masses must include inculcation of true standards of financial, social and economic value above all things.

Varied Aspects of Life :

Man is a complex being; we cannot divide him up into water-tight compartments and develop him in stages. Education, which attends only to the intellectual development, leaving aside the physical, moral and spiritual aspects, is directed towards the production of monstrosities. If our aim is a true education, we have to attend to all faculties at one and the same time. We have to develop a person physically, socially, mentally and spiritually. He has to learn an occupation, he has to learn how to live as a member of a community, he has to know how to evaluate men and matters. Unless all these are attempted we can have no education worth the name.

There is not a single action of ours that does not leave its indelible mark on us. Our work, our play, our pastime, and our rest all have to be consciously planned out if the reactions have to be healthy socially. Training for work takes care of the major part of a worker's life. We spend most of our time in our economic activity. If it is so arranged that it develops our faculties and enriches our life in the process of producing goods, to that extent the nation will be the better for it. Proper work will not wear out a nation but build it. The function of work should be to practise our ideal of life. Pure religion which begins and ends with ceremonial worship is superficial. If religion does not affect every act of ours, every moment of our life, it is futile. We have seen by our analysis of work, in the chapter on the Function of Work, the highly important role that work plays in developing the individual and the race. If work can be so potent a force in developing the adult, we can well harness it to develop the child.

Finance and Organization :

The present system of Government finance, which makes education depend upon the revenue from excise is a political strategy. It is fundamentally wrong in principle. We need not burn the thatching of the poor to prepare tea for the children of the middle classes. It impoverishes the poor, ruins their family life and destroys their character to add a little butter to the middle classes. No nation can march on to progress on the blood of its masses. It is better to be without such education than to murder the fathers and prostitute the mothers so that we may provide cheap clerks to the Government. Let us cry a halt and take stock of the situation. We shall then see our way clear to plan a healthy system of mass education which will create without destroying, produce health without death, add to our wealth without resorting to robbery. Let those of us, who have received more than our share, give freely to those who stand in need. Life is enriched not by what we possess but by what we give to others in a spirit of service. A well with a good spring becomes purer and purer by greater quantities of water being drawn from it.

We have to concentrate our efforts on the villages. University education can go overboard for a time without damaging the nation. As it is we are top-heavy, we have many more graduates than we need. These have also created a problem of unemployment as they are not products of the type of education we need. Otherwise, there would be no difficulty in absorbing them. Our end must be to make our villagers more useful and efficient. It is not necessary to load them with much outside information. Radio and talkies, though they may be helpful, cannot be the main source of rural education. The amount spent on them is disproportionately high. The work must be an evolution from within the village and not an imposition from outside the community. Anything from outside will require to be propped up by artificial means but that which comes from within will develop true culture which will bind man to man, village to village and ultimately the country itself as one whole.

We need not place too much emphasis on the organization to be brought into existence. When we pin our faith on organizations, however important they may be in themselves, we often lose sight of the personal influence and the organization tends to become expensive and wooden. Centralization of education, as in other spheres, leads to too much control from those at a distance. Centralization of education will lead to hide-bound methods and standardization which are fatal to true education. It is much better for the village teacher to work under the eyes of his neighbours. Therefore, it would seem better if each village can be made to finance its own education by the old method of endowing lands to a *Mandir* dedicated to education. If such a system can have the advantage of inspection and advice from the centre, it ought to answer our purpose well, as the management itself will be amenable to local public opinion. As it is, the teacher has to satisfy the inspector once a year or so and after such inspection is over, he relaxes. This does not make for progress, much less for steady work. Every village school should be the centre of culture and the point of contact with the outside world. The only danger this conception is that the teacher may get into the habit of looking upon his part in the village as one of promoting social spirit and may neglect his main duty to the younger generation. This social aspect is only a bye-product, it is not the end of a school. Let us place our faith in human nature and in ourselves and go ahead keeping our lode-star in sight. We may differ in details, but we shall reach our goal of developing true culture, reliable standards of value and attain unity in spite of our apparent diversity.

The Suggested Scheme :

Of late there has been a good deal of discussion as to the line which true education should take. Gandhiji suggests education should be made self-supporting. He writes, "By education I mean an all-round drawing out of the best in child and man—body, mind and spirit. Literacy is not the end of education nor even the beginning. It is only one of the means whereby man and woman can be educated. Literacy in itself is no education. I would, therefore, begin with the child's education by teaching it a useful handicraft enabling it to produce from the moment it begins its training. Thus, every school can be made self-supporting, the condition being that the State takes over the manufactures of these schools.

"I hold that the highest development of the mind and the soul is possible under such a system of education. Only every such handicraft has to be taught not merely mechanically, as is done today, but scientifically, *i. e.*, the child should know the way and the wherefore of every process. I am not writing this without some confidence, because it has the backing of experience. This method is being adopted more or less completely wherever spinning is being taught to workers. I have myself taught sandal-making and even spinning on these lines with good results. This method does not exclude a knowledge of history and geography. But I find this is best taught by transmitting such general information by word of mouth. One imparts ten times as much in this manner as by reading and writing. The signs of the alphabet may be taught later when he has somewhat developed his or her tastes. This is a revolutionary proposal but it saves immense labour and enables a student to acquire in one year what he may take much longer to learn. This means all-round economy. Of course the pupil learns mathematics whilst he is learning his handicraft.

"I attach the greatest importance to primary education which, according to my conception, should be equal to the present matriculation less English. If all the collegians were all of a sudden to forget their knowledge, the loss sustained by the sudden lapse of the memory of say a few lacs of collegians would be as nothing compared to the loss that the nation has sustained and is sustaining through the ocean of darkness that surrounds three hundred millions. The measure of illiteracy is no adequate measure of the prevailing ignorance among the millions of villagers."

The education of children in the early stages can never be self-supporting. The articles they may produce will not command any exchange value. If the State is to take them over that will only be another way of meeting the loss and we shall be deceiving ourselves that education is self-supporting. What Gandhiji means by self-supporting is not that each year of the child must be paid for by the products that the child makes in that year. This is too narrow a financial viewpoint and it can never be true. What is meant is a much wider value, not in terms of money only, but in terms of future services rendered by the child as a well-trained citizen. At present frequently the drilling in the three Rs. that a child gets in a village, is so feeble that after a few years it lapses into illiteracy again and the time and money spent on the child become a sheer waste in course of time. But if it has been properly spent, the production of the class, though it may not pay for itself each year, in the course of the seven years' schooling, the aggregate production of the class ought to cover the amount spent on the salary of the teacher. In the first two years it may just balance and the last two years, if the child had been properly trained, ought to show a profit sufficient to cover the losses of the first two years.. Apart from this, as has already been pointed out, the training of a good citizen more than compensates any capital expense incurred by the State. When the child is taught crafts which are in local demand such as spinning, dyeing, weaving, tailoring, mat and basket-making, pottery, shoe-making, carpentry, smithy, brass and metal working, paper-making, gur production, oil-pressing, bee-keeping etc., the problem of marketing will not be great. Even the apprentice of an artisan does not pay for himself from the very start. His training is bound to result in a loss for some-time. After the initial stages, he may produce something worthwhile. Thence onwards he may pay his training. To meet such early training the Government has to find the funds or the people will have to set aside certain assets like lands earmarked for the purpose. This was done formerly until the British system of taxation dis-established the village schools. But education of the young must remain a duty of the State. As we are situated at present, our problem is a politically created financial problem and is not natural. The solution lies in correcting it politically and not accepting it as inevitable. The teacher should himself be a well-trained person who may have to be paid adequately say Rs. 25/- as a start. The school hours and terms should be related to the village calendar. There may be no classes during harvest seasons or during periods when a great deal of work has to be done on the fields.

General Outline of the Plan :

The Wardha or Basic scheme, as this new plan has come to be known, recommends a course of seven years' compulsory basic education for boys and girls from the age seven to fourteen. The medium of instruction is to be a craft, like spinning, around which all subjects are taught. The everyday life of the child and the correlation of the craft, the physical and social environment of the child afford points of co-ordination for all departments of knowledge. The standard aimed at is the present matriculation without English. There will be no effort to teach writing until the child has learnt drawing. Reading will be taught first. After the age of twelve, the pupil may be allowed to choose a craft as a vocation. It does not aim at turning out expert workmen at the age of fourteen, but the pupil will have acquired sufficient training to enter a vocation in which he will do his talents justice.

The central idea of this scheme is that intellectual development must be attained through vocational training. The present system emphasises general education and bases vocational training on it. Therefore, when intellectual training comes first, we, in a way, tie the hands and feet of the child and he becomes impractical. No amount of the latter training will ever restore his limbs paralysed in childhood. Instruction without experience to base it on, becomes a pure memory training exercise. It does not develop any initiative or personality.

Examination :

The brunt of examinations will be borne by the teaching staff and not by the pupils under this scheme. As the pupil's life is to be controlled by the teacher for 24 hours, of the day, the teacher becomes knit together with the home of every child and so with the village. The work of the teacher will be reflected in the condition of the homes and of the villager.

Women's Part :

We have to follow the natural physical development of the child and follow it mentally, morally and spiritually. The child takes interest in form, colour and movement and then tries to understand the reason why things are what they are. Then he will experiment to see if he cannot make things what he wants them to be. Thus he advances from play to investigation and then to creation. Our educational system has to cater for these three stages of growth if we plan on eliciting the best in each child. To do this the teacher ought to be fully qualified to enter into the spirit of the child and share it with him. By temperament and natural endowment, women, generally speaking, are better able to understand children of the first stage. The system in India suffers in no small measure by the lack of education among women. The mothers are not qualified to train the child nor can we get properly educated young women to enter the schools as teachers. It seems to me if we are to reform the schools, the first step is the education of girls and young women, who are the natural custodians of the generations to come. Unless we begin there, any amount of planning and scheming by mere man will be in vain as he only comes in after the impressionable age of the child has been lost. Every village school, handling children under eight, must be in the hands of women. One can almost say that with rare exceptions no man teacher should be employed in such schools.

In the second stage of development of the child, we need persons who will stimulate the thinking of the pupils and explain the why and wherefore of phenomena. I had the opportunity of visiting a school in New York State run by the Federation of Labour Unions. In that school the whole community lived together and the children took part in the supply of food products and all other domestic matters. They had their own dairy; one of the teachers was in charge and a few boys helped him. I attended an "Economic Class" of pupils of about eleven years of age. The subject for the day was "Buying of a Cow". The class was taken charge of by a boy of about ten; the teacher sat in a back row with me. The lad in charge (we shall call him Henry) described to the class what his experience was when he went with the teacher (Bill) in charge of the Dairy to an adjoining market to buy a cow. This is how the class went on : "Bill and I went to an auction to buy a cow because we do not get enough milk from our cow for us all". One of the pupils asked what an "auction" was. The other explained "An auction is a shop whrere they had no fixed prices. The shopmen brought out an article and the persons who wanted it told him what they would pay for it and the shopman gave it to the one who "bid highest". Then followed an explanation what a 'bid' was. Then another pupil asked why different persons 'bid' different prices. Henry replied, "The cow they bought started at 75 dollars and was 'knocked down' at 120 dollars for Bill". After that explanation of "knocked down" he said that the first man suggested paying 75 dollars and other went on increasing the price till Bill bid 120 dollars. After that nobody came forward with a higher price, so it was sold to Bill. Another pupil asked, "Why nobody wanted to give more than 120 dollars ?" Henry described how before the auction all the prospective buyers had gone through the records of the cow and found how much milk per year it gave, what food it ate during the year and other costs and found out what amount spent on its price would be just covered by the price of milk. So the highest limit was calculated and those who wanted an animal would stop bidding when it reached this limit. The whole hour spent by those children in thinking these things out for themselves stimulated their faculties to a greater extent than the cramming of economic theories from Adam Smith to Marshall. When theories are based on experience, it leads gently on to the next stage of creation and originality.

The present system is not capable of producing origianal thinkers. Even Graduates of our universities have reached this third stage. It is because of this defect that we are stagnating. As we have already seen, the instruction we were given was designed to make clerks of us and an original mind is no part of the equipment of a clerk. This stage requires some initiative and a good deal of self-confidence. The part the teachers should play is to stand by, watch and suggest.

No vocational training or education can be complete unless it has some relation to art. This part of our education has been attended to by Poet Tagore. The emphasis placed on folk songs, music and art must form part of every village school. If such schools can be found to function with a vocation or craft as the base and art as an aid, however simple the courses may be, the result will be an out-turn of men and women with a backbone of character and self-respect who will not purr round the feet of foreign masters for a silken couch to lie on, but who will hold their head erect, be independent, and be prepared to share the lowly life of the general run of the people. Unless we bend all our might to produce such a stalwart nation, broad-based on the sound culture of the masses, it will be futile to attempt to build a superstructure. No nation can ever hope to take its place in the vanguard of the nations which has not got its roots in its own culture. We cannot shine on borrowed feathers. We have to develop our own contribution to the world of literature, art and music.

Of course, as Gandhiji suggested, college education must be made self-supporting. An agricultural college, which cannot maintain itself on the land allotted to it, belies the object for which it exists. Similarly, all other professional and technical colleges should be made to pay for themselves.

CHAPTER 19 * DEMOCRACY IN THE ORIENT

When democratic constitution-making is in the air, as at present in our country, it will be well to consider briefly the principles on which democracy is based and the attempts made at various times to attain it.

We are familiar with the words of that liberator of mankind, Abraham Lincoln : "Government of the people, by the people and for the people." Sir John Seely in dealing with a much narrower sense of the word explained it as "Government in which everyone has a share," and A. V. Dicey saw democracy where "the groverning body is a comparatively large fraction of the entire nation." All these had in mind merely the political aspect of the application of the principle of democracy.

Democratic ideals however, do not begin and end with politics. If this were all, then democracy would dwindle into a state of, as Lord Bryce observes, "the physical force of the citizens with their voting power" and this would mean dictatorship in effect. The true seeds of democracy, on the other hand, sprout and blossom forth in every walk of life. In our examination of the subject, we shall accordingly extend our observations to the religious, social and economic spheres as well.

If democracy is to pervade the whole life of a people, it is obvious that it must not be founded merely on the exigencies

* Reprinted from the '*Aryan Path*' by courtesy of the Editors.

of politics but on eternal principles. During the French Revolution, an attempt was made to derive democracy from such principles and it expressed itself in the slogan "Liberty, Equality and Fraternity." If these three principles are to be applied in practice, an order of Society will have to be devised in which their working out will not lead to conflict between individuals. Liberty for instance, cannot be absolute. Every person will have to surrender a part of his liberty for the benefit of society and ultimately, it will prove to be for his own benefit also. Nor is perfect equality possible as long as there are differences in nature, so also fraternity cannot be understood in the literal sense of the world.

In a true democracy, society should be so planned as to allow full scope for the development of the individual and yet should establish a relative equality by helping and safeguarding the interests of the weak, thus forming a brotherhood in which no one can exploit another. The whole social structure should represent the ideal of progress of all the component parts. Democracy vanishes the moment any one person or group of persons obtains a dominating position. The satisfactory working of its mechanism must be baseed not on sanctions originating from violence, might or money power but from a desire inculcated in the masses to realize the eternal principles of Justice, Truth, Non-Violence and Love. The working of such a system will then be automatic, impersonal and unobtrusive.

To attain such a democracy, the ideals will have to be assimilated subconsciously by society, if we may use language suggestive of the view of society as an organism. A person who is learning to ride a bicycle, controls his bodily movements by conscious effort. His brain is at the helm. As the brain is not quick enough to give immediate effect to change of direction, his progress is jerky and irregular. An expert cyclist, on the other hand, is not even conscious of being on a bicycle. The control has passed from his brain to his nervous system. It functions almost automatically without any effort and more quickly than conscious thought. Hence he rides gracefully and in a perfect straight line. In the same way, if society is to fulfil its purposes smoothly and without periodical upheavals, the control must be from the inner self and not from outside. Such a state we may call "cultural democracy."

The amateur cyclist's control is functional, as his faculties have consciously to guide his movements. So also where democratic principles have not permeated into the very being of the people and the community is guided by one or a few individuals at the helm, the direction is from outside, and therefore, does not work automatically. It may have the outward form, but lacks the inward urge. We may term such a state "functional democracy". *We may create functional democracies overnight, but cultural democracies are products of millennia. Only the latter will stand the test of time.*

The essence of functional democracy is the form based on a widely diffused franchise. Cultural democracy, on the other hand, is based on the will of the people themselves which finds expression, not in mere votes, but in actual administrative power. Just as the majority of persons refrain from stealing, not because they fear jail, but because they have cultivated an inborn respect for other persons' rights, so when every individual, of his own accord, desires the social good and acts accordingly, we shall have attained cultural democracy—which needs no voting constituencies, but in which the executive power can devolve on each individual to a limited extent.

When we survey the races of mankind and trace the development of democracies, we find an interesting sequence according to their maturity and environment.

The warmer climate of Southern Europe conduced to social life and aggregation in clustering huts of villages. These produced the city civilization of Greece and Rome. But the black Northern and Western parts of Europe led to the development of isolated farmsteads emphasising individuality. Under such circumstances, we should expect to find seasonal leadership with strong discipline and unquestioning obedience. With this tradition, is it natural to form so called democractic parliamentary governments where the number of votes count more than their quality, Similarly in religion, the organization in the West tapers upwards to the Pope; in social life to the Courts or Kings, and in economics to the capitalist. As long as such small groups provide the leadership, there are bound to be conflicts of interest and these democracies are little different from dictatorships whether of an individual or of a small group. In fact, if we scratch the surface of such democracies, we shall find the tribal chieftain with a garland of skulls. With the crust removed we meet Mussolinis and Hitlers. With the crust removed, we have the Cabinet in England tied to the apron strings of financiers. The man in the street has hardly any real part in the Government. Such democracies flourish on the ignorance of the public which is spoonfed. The leading group or class keeps itself apart by its etiquette, decorum and cultivated social manners which form a divisive factor rather than an adhesive force as far as the masses are concerned.

As in the case of the "Good Samaritan", real democracy and true culture should help to bridge over racial and other barriers. Western 'democracy' however, accentuates differences according to group allegiances. At present we see geographical, ethnical and religious divisions amongst nations and class differences within nations. Thus it has been possible to set nation against nation and class against class and so produce an unstable equilibrium to maintain a balance of power. As Bertrand Russell states : "England has hitherto been the decisive factor in preserving that state of anarchy which our grandfathers called "the liberties of Europe." Even a socialist of the rank of Karl Marx believes that tropical countries are legitimate booty for European states because of the latter's "superior civilization." How shall we find "Liberty, Equality and Fraternity" where such provincialism prevails and where, in consequence, even motherhood has been converted into an ammunition factory ? Naturally personal or group Governments such as these, which emphasise narrow loyalties and divide up peoples, give rise to conflicts resulting in international strife. The same is the position even in religion in the West. The hankering for converts and the missionary crusade against other religions is the outcome of such unconscious group loyalty.

As we move towards the East, we come to Islamic Democracy. This has definitely left the primitive and functional type and advanced in the cultural stage of democracy. Here the life of the people is not conditioned by the dictates of a single individual or of a group but by the functioning of a socio-religious order which has sought to bring "Liberty, Equality and Fraternity" to the prince and the peasant, the sage and the savage, the black and white. It has attained almost an international rank but for the limit of a common allegiance to the Prophet of Mecca. The social, the economic, the political, the ethnical and geographical barriers have been let down but the religious frontier remains impregnable.

Similarly in China and Japan (as she was before reverting to the functional type half a century ago) we find the cultural form of democracy. Just as Islamic Democracy was limited by religion, so the Mongolian Democracy fell short of the ideal by a certain amount of feudalism and racial isolation. Within such limitation the life of the nation was ordered by a social organization very similar to what we observe in our own land. This cultural organization is impersonal and performs its duty irrespective of the individual concerned. When Bertrand Russell advocates the formation of large self-contained states to avoid international conflict, he is moving towards the Mongolian type of democracy.

In our own country, we get a picture of the political life of the people from the old *Nitisastras* and *Puranas*. The daily life of the people is still ordered and regulated, not by external pressure but by the functioning of a socio-religious economic order which has become a part of the people themselves. It is this that holds together the diverse elements that compose our continent. Westerners, who look at us through their functional democracy, see divisive factors in language, customs and geographical conditions and declare we have neither unity nor political sense, as our people do not seem capable of blindly following a leader or party, which quality is a *sine qua non* for the satisfactory working of functional democracy. And yet a fairly advanced form of a really democratic type of Government, well on the way to realizing the full cultural democracy indicated above, is to be found in our ancient village administration. In a cultural democracy physical differences, such as race, colour or territory are not capable of making lasting impressions. Our system was so virile and cosmopolitan that it found no difficulty in absorbing even invaders and foreigners. As already said, the principles of this democracy have been woven into the life and thought of the people through the ages by means of social regulations and institutions. If there are Kings, they are but minor wheels in the machinery and according to *Sukra Niti*, they are but glorified policemen and legislators. The real Government is in the hands of the people. Decentralized small bodies, the village panchayats, decide on matters vitally affecting the local community. The authority of the panchayats, depends on the confidence placed in it by the people, a confidence based on close personal knowledge of the members composing it, and its sanction is not imprisonment but the power to declare the offender a *gramadrohin* (traitor to the village). Its decisions are not majority decisions but are made unanimous by winning over the dissenting minority. Such a Government may be truly said to function from within as the actual administrative decision is in the hands of the people themselves.

A centralized Government, on the other hand, cannot be a Government by the people and rarely can it be a Government for the people. *If the Government is to be by the people, it must reach down to the meanest village. No mere enlargement of the franchise, however broadbased, will ever answer the purpose.*

Further, no group, however detached, can function in an impartial way in matters in which its interests conflict with the interests of others. Such matters require detachment in time as well, and should be regulated by means of impersonal regulations and institutions as in our ancient form of Government. By so doing, the interests of the weak and the poor will be safeguarded. The joint family system, for example, was an attempt at a modification of distribution and at providing for the less efficient members of society. The *Baluta* system of payment in kind was a device to ensure a minimum means of subsistence to everyone. There was not a department of life that was not thus provided for. India had attained such a cultural democracy centuries ago. But for its impersonal decentralized working, our civilization could not have withstood the manigold vicissitudes of life to this day. When the purity of such conception in a cultural democracy was affected by the introduction of inequalities and discriminations, and when the duties of the custodians of culture faded away into the rights of privileged classes, the seeds of decay took root and India fell a victim to foreign invaders.

Decentralization, which was as the basis of our democracy, was the great principle worked out by our people in all walks of life. Even in religion, it will not be possible to find a more decentralized and therefore, necessarily tolerant form of thought, action and worship than Hinduism. The social order was governed by the *Varnashram dharma*, which meant that each individual's duty was determined by his unique place in the community. In the economic sphere, where people were endowed differently by nature, the practice of *laissez-faire* led to exploitation of the weak by the strong. This tendency was curbed and competition modified by the conception of division of labour under the caste system.

Thus, by checks and counter-checks laid down by consideration of fundamental principles, *India had arrived at a formula which approximated real cultural democracy and the Government it had evolved was truly a Government of the villagers, and for the villagers.*

Yet there was one drawback. According to the *Varnashrama dharma* it is only by conforming to the divine and eternal plan of performing the duties incidental to ones position in the community that one can obtain freedom. The individual by himself counts for little. Any value that may be attached to him comes from his being a member of the society. He is like the drop of water that goes to make a beautiful waterfall. The drop of water passes away but the waterfall is a lasting factor. Individual interests are not supreme. It is society that matters, and its welfare is to be sought irrespective of the inconvenience it may cause to the individual. In an ideal democracy, however, the individual cannot thus be minimised, for it is he that constitutes society and it is his development that is the goal of all human endeavour. When we obtain such a form of society where the scope of the individual for full development of his personality is not restricted, and where in developing himself he develops others, we shall have attained the ideal human state.

Our consideration shows that Western democracies are still at the stage where nations are led by small groups or individuals and where sanctions are based on violence. Eastern democracies have passed over to the cultural stage but they also have fallen short of real democracy in so far as they have only reached religious or village units and have not got down to individuals. When the world advances to the stage where every one functions according to the ideals inculcated and performs his *Swadharma*, and the sanctions are based on love and truth, then we shall have projected Lincoln's ideal of functional democracy on to the cultural form and obtained a self-acting democracy which will be a Government of the person, by the person and for the person; and this, in the aggregate, will materialise into a Government of the people, by the people and for the people.

CHAPTER 20 INTERNATIONAL PEACE

We have considered in the sixth chapter various factors which lead to strife amongst nations. We traced the seeds of dissention to the methods of economic production and the difficulties consequent on supplies preceding demand. In the subsequent chapters, we discussed methods of production, which distribute economic activities amongst the masses. Where there is decentralization of this type, it is not possible for such small producers to combine and create a menace to international peace. Raw materials will be exploited in the locality in which they are found and the products will also be disposed of amongst the people. If there is any international trade, it will be of small magnitude, and it will not entail the necessity of controlling the source of raw materials. Nor will the supplies, which will be scattered and small, require "the civilizing of backward races" in order to sell them. Supplies will follow a natural demand, and no violence will be needed to equate the two. Every man will get the fruits of his own labour however small it may be, and there will be no opportunity provided to make one wealthy at the cost of another with the aid of violence. If women control demand, production will follow a natural course, and we shall not witness a world glutted with one kind of commodity while it lacks others. Nor shall we have to resort to violence to establish equilibrium. Man will realise his inner urge for self-expression in his work, and no violence will be needed to whip him on to further effort. Nor will there be any need to control raw material sources or markets with violence. A sense of human values will direct economic activity into right channels. Such being the case, we shall render impotent the causes which are at the root of international rivalry, jealousies and competition. In so far as these causes are removed, or in the proportion in which they are minimised, the chances of war breaking out will also have been controlled. If this can be achieved, it will lead to human progress, peace and the prosperity of all nations.

The Non-Violent Way :

If we wish to abandon war, we have to arrange our economic order in such a way that it does not require periodical upheavals to put right its working. Man is higher than the beast only in the measure in which he has abandoned violence in his life. People are civilized in the inverse ratio of the extent to which they utilize violence. Since the days of Buddha India has held up non-violence as an ideal. The Hindus have attained a mellowness of maturity in their culture which will eschew with disdain all use of violence in human relations. Might is not going to rule the world notwithstanding all appearances to the contrary. Mammoths and dinosaurs with all their gigantic muscles, have had to yield place to the feeble but intellectual man. So also the cultural and spiritual forces will dispel the powers of evil which seem to hold sway today. If we desire to usher in a world set and organized for peace and goodwill there is no other way but to control our greed and curb our avarice. To achieve this on a nation wide scale it is imperative that the profit motive must be sterilised from large scale production by reserving all centralized industries to the ownership and control of the State. Handicrafts and cottage industries are non-violent in a large measure, and can be left with impunity in the hands of private individuals even with the incentive to profit, as it has its own limitations and does not lend itself to exploitation generally. May be, life in such a society cannot be based on a multiplicity of wants, but there are other considerations much more vital than material possessions.

INDEX

BOOKS BY Dr. J. C. KUMARAPPA

Principles and Studies

1. Why the Village Movement ? ... 3—00
2. Economy of Permanence ... 3—00
3. Gandhian Economic Thought ... 1—25
4. Gandhian way of life ... 0—75
5. Public Finance and Our Poverty ... 1—50
6. Report on the Financial Obligation between Great Britain and India. (with Kumarappa as Convener) 1931 (out of print)
7. Clive to Keynes ... 0—75
8. Organisation and Accounts of Relief Work ... 1—00
9. An Overall Plan for Rural Development ... 1—50
10. Unitary Basis for Non-violent Democracy ... 0—63
11. Currency Inflation: Its Cause and Cure ... 0—75

Travels

12. People's China: What I Saw and Learnt There ... 0—75
13. Report on Agriculture, Cottage and Small-scale Industries in Japan ... 1—25
14. A Peep Behind the Iron Curtain ... 1—50
15. Lessons from Europe ... 0—50

Surveys

16. Survey of Matar Taluka - 1931 ... 4—00
17. Report of the Industrial Survey Committee of C.P. and Berar (with Kumarappa as Chairman) 1939 ... 3—00
18. A Plan for the Economic Development of North-West Frontier Province 1940 ... 0—81
19. Report of the Congress Agrarian Reforms Committee (with Kumarappa as Chairman) 1948 ... 5—00

Religion

20. Practice and Precepts of Jesus ... 1—50
21. Christianity : Its Economy and Way of life ... 1—25

Essays

22. Philosophy of work and other Essays ... 0—75

23. Gandhian Economy and other Essays ... 2—50
24. Science and Progress ... 1—00
25. Peace and Prosperity ... 1—00
26. Swaraj for the Masses ... 1—00
27. Blood Money ... 0—75
28. Present Economic Situation ... 2—00
29. Our Food Problem ... 1—50
30. Banishing War ... 0—50
31. Non-Violent Economy and World Peace ... 1—00
32. Sarvodaya and World Peace ... 0—13
33. Planning for the People by the People ... 3—00
34. Women and Village Industries ... 0—1
35. Cow in our Economy ... 0—7
36. Vicarious Living ... 0—7

Biographical

37. Stone walls and Iron Bars ... 0—5

By others

38. The Economics of Peace : The Cause and the Man (S. K. George and G. Ramachandran) ... 10—0
39. J.C. Kumarappa and His Quest for World Peace (M. Vinaik) ... 1—5
40. Sarvodaya & Electricity ... 0—7